*For Felix*

# ABOUT THE AUTHOR

Caroline Scheuermann has twelve years' experience bringing up an ADHD son. Using her experience, she now runs her own consultancy business helping support families who are struggling to cope. Her background in science has helped her when reading and learning about the fascinating condition ADHD. Now the mother of three children she and her family, four cats and four chickens lives happily in Kent.

# INTRODUCTION

Attention Deficit Hyperactivity Disorder (ADHD) was first described more than 100 years ago. The positive effects of medication have been known for over half a century.

ADHD is not an epidemic and occurs no more frequently now than it has historically, we are simply better at recognising the symptoms, which is a good thing. The condition affects approximately 20 % of the population, which means in a class of thirty children it could be expected that up to six children will have ADHD to some extent or another. ADHD is a spectrum condition and will vary in its severity and characteristics. It is strongly inheritable and can usually it can be traced in families.

When a parent suspects something is not quite right, they are usually correct, the phrase 'Mum knows best' is very true here. It can be hard if you only have a single child, or if this is your eldest child. First suspicions will most likely be that a parent will notice subtle differences in their child's development and behaviour compared to their peer group. In spite of the quality of parental input and interventions the problems will persist and become more obvious over time. The parent at this stage might seek help, but if a child is preschool, they will most likely to be told to wait and see. This is the right approach as all children develop differently and at their own pace. If problems persist the parents will need to seek external help.

There are a lot of self-styled experts who will voice their opinion to the parents and it can be a mine field to know where to start. I remember with my own child that I knew something was amiss by the time he was 18 months old. He was wild, wilful, he would bite (seemingly at random), he would become extremely overstimulated and took a long time to calm down. He did not sleep well and would awaken frequently. Friends would say "it's just a phase" or that their child was just like him and grew out of it. This might have been true, but he wasn't like them, he didn't grow out of it, if anything he got worse and with the volume turned up.

As a toddler, other children did not warm to him—and that's understating it. In short, he was high maintenance, always on the go, always talking and although I loved him, I was exhausted and confused by him. When his little brother was born, it threw into sharp relief the differences in the two children highlighting further my older son's difficulties and differences.

The problems became more and more obvious as he got older, preschool adopted the typical wait and see approach. By the time he was in reception class it was blindingly obvious, yet it was still me who had to be the driving force behind his diagnosis; school were still saying he was very young and a boy—I could wait no longer. We were both by this stage miserable and having moved countries, we were both friendless, isolated and lonely.

There is a demonstratable difference in normal brain function that causes a clever child to underachieve academically and have poor behaviour in spite of having high quality parenting. This difference in brain function is caused by an imbalance in the neurotransmitters dopamine and noradrenaline. The parts of the brain affected are the frontal lobes and the basal ganglia circuits, which are responsible for self-monitoring and -regulation.

ADHD can be classed as inattentive, hyperactive or the combined type. To qualify for a diagnosis a child must be over six years old and be significantly out of step with others at the same developmental level and quality of parenting. Symptoms must be overserved for at least six months in two or more settings, e.g., school or home. The child must also meet many of the diagnostic criteria as outlined in the DSM-V.

At school, ADHD presents the majority of its problems in two different ways:

- The hyperactive-impulsive behaviours mean that a child might rush through their work, settle slowly, fidget, tap, irritate, annoy, call out and disrupt. This leads to social impairment and missed learning opportunities.
- The attention deficit problems lead to poor organisation, slow to get started, poor listening and recall skills, inability to sustain a constant level or work output, easily distracted and a weak short-term memory. This has impacts on the most fundamental aspects of primary school, such as times tables recall, weekly spelling tests and comprehension skills to name but a few.

Many ADHD children are socially impaired and immature; typically, they behave like children who are 3-5years below their chronological age. This means in a year six class an 11-year-old ADHD child might have the social skills of a 6-year-old. They are often sort out by bullies as they are easy to victimise and often overreact to teasing. They are often verbally and physically accident prone. Their impulsive behaviours make these children and adults more vulnerable to manipulation and exploitation.

It is the aim of this book to empower parents, teachers and caregivers by giving practical strategies to help families and children so that they can be successful.

ADHD is diagnosed by the presence of:

*A persistent pattern of inattention and/or hyperactivity-impulsivity that interferes with functioning or development, as characterised by*:

Inattention: Six (or more) of the following symptoms have persisted for at least 6 months to a degree that is inconsistent with developmental level and that negatively impacts directly on social and academic/occupational activities. For adolescents and adults (age 17 and older), at least five symptoms are required.

a. Often fails to give close attention to details or makes careless mistakes in schoolwork, at work, or during other activities.

b. Often has difficulty sustaining attention in tasks or play activities.

c. Often does not seem to listen when spoken to directly.

d. Often does not follow through on instructions and fails to finish schoolwork or duties in the workplace.

e. Often has difficulty organizing tasks.

f. Often avoids, dislikes, or is reluctant to engage in tasks that require sustained mental effort.

g. Often loses things necessary for tasks or activities.

h. Is often easily distracted by extraneous stimuli.

i. Is often forgetful in daily activities.

2. Hyperactivity and impulsivity: Six (or more) of the following symptoms have persisted for at least 6 months to a degree that is inconsistent with developmental level and that negatively impacts directly on social and academic/occupational activities. For older adolescents and adults (age 17 and older), at least five symptoms are required.

a. Often fidgets with or taps hands or feet or squirms in seat.

b. Often leaves seat in situations when remaining seated is expected.

c. Often runs about or climbs in situations where it is inappropriate.

d. Often unable to play or engage in leisure activities quietly.

e. Is often "on the go," acting as if "driven by a motor".

f. Often talks excessively.

g. Often blurts out an answer before a question has been completed.

h. Often has difficulty waiting his or her turn.

i. Often interrupts or intrudes on others.

ADHD is not a problem that is exclusive to boys, girls can have it too. However typically it does present differently in girls and is, sadly, often not diagnosed until later in life. Girls tend to be less hyperactive, boisterous and problematic to many but themselves. They still struggle with friendships, inattention (they are often described as daydreamers), they can be controlling of their environment and very talkative (appearing as bossy and busybodies). Both boys and girls typically can't understand what they do to make others dislike them and typically suffer from very low self-esteem. Both boys and girls have significant problems with organisation and remaining focused on tasks that require sustained mental effort. They frequently struggle to rest and get enough sleep. With age the symptoms of ADHD can change, often the hyperactive element dissipates, but the other problems will remain an impairment for the individual.

# WHAT ADHD DOES
# TO A FAMILY

ADHD is an incredibly inheritable neurobiological condition.[1] It is life-long and typically evolves over time wreaking havoc in families, decimating careers and leaving the individual socially isolated and vulnerable; if left untreated. It is estimated on average that children with ADHD receive approximately 20,000 more negative comments from their peer group by age 10 than those who do not have the condition.[2] Symptoms, such as the hyperactive element can dissipate over time, however impulsivity and inattention remain significant impairments.

These symptoms often manifest themselves as poor time keeping, time management which leads to anxiety and depression as well as poor impulse control. It is therefore obvious that these individuals are more often passed over for promotion at work, or even out of work. Relationships fall by the way side as anniversaries are forgotten, hyper-focus means they forget it's parents' evening and the cleaning and shopping are not achieved—but the all-important super car magazines have been alphabetically sorted and ordered chronologically. To the untrained eye their behaviour appears selfish to say the least, in reality the ADHD mind has become side-tracked.

If the mundane tasks fall on the non-ADHD spouse, it can feel like there is an extra child is in the household. It has to be noted that this extra "child" is capable of very great things, but time management is not one of them.

It can be incredibly frustrating for the non-ADHD person to co-exist with someone with ADHD, like an overgrown toddler who can reach the sugar and means to help but does not see the detritus in their wake. It's little wonder that so many of these unions collapse, not because the ADHD-er is not loveable or likable, but the chaos that co-exists is often unbearable. Divorce rates for ADHD couples are estimated to be twice that of their neurotypical counterparts.[3]

Friends are likely to be transient for similar reasons, "flaky" behaviour, like forgetting gatherings and hyper-focusing on specific topics all can lead to eventual ostracization. ADHD people can have a tendency to talk lots, while at the same time appearing not to listen to others' points of view. Naturally this is off putting for many prospective friends and partners. These features are often exacerbated further if the ADHD person feels stressed or anxious.

Having an ADHD child in the family—even without co existing parental ADHD—can wreak the same havoc. Friends and family can be judgemental about the child's behaviour labelling them as naughty and the parents as weak or ineffective. Alternatively, a parent can be told they are too strict, too rigid and controlling and naturally this is the cause of their child's difficulties. Siblings can be side-lined as the ADHD child often requires so much more attention. Invitations to family and friends' events start to dwindle and the parent feels socially isolated and in a, often sleepless, fog not knowing what to do to help themselves. Siblings feel resentful of the child and the parents and this just compounds the problems further until the situation feels untenable and chaotic. People with ADHD, as a result of societies misunderstanding of them, often have very low self-esteem, and are more likely to suffer from anxiety and depression.

It would be hoped that school could offer some form of advice, support and a refuge for such families. Sometimes this can be true, but more often than not it is a similar story. This time professionals label the child as naughty and the parents weak and ineffective or overly sensitive and neurotic. Often, teachers do not know how ADHD can present in the classroom because they have only a very rudimentary training in many areas of SEND.

Having a diagnosis should make this situation easier. However, there still exists the myth that ADHD is an excuse for poor, even bad, behaviour that can be helped when the child wants to do something they are really engaged in. It can be a lottery to see if you get the school that is understanding and compassionate towards an ADHD child and really believes that this is a condition that the child cannot help. Even in the most understanding institutions there will usually be at least one teacher, which undoubtedly will be your class teacher, who still believes the "myth". This can lead to missed opportunities in learning, a significant gap in performance and ability and erosion of a child's self-esteem along with social isolation from the peer group.

It is not unusual that party and tea invitations dry up by the time a child reaches Year 1 in primary school and that social isolation and ostracization starts from this young age. The child is labelled as a naughty by the teacher, this feeds home to the parents, *via* five- and six-year-old children, who watch in horror as the ADHD child emerges from school like a wild creature released from the zoo. The cohort's parents like their ornaments and house as they are, so they shepherd their children away and walk home quietly; leaving the ADHD child and their family alone. This treatment can have a detrimental impact on siblings too, as they find themselves ostracised in the playground and from social events serving only to fuel the family divisions further.

I will always remember one sunny summer Sunday afternoon; our family had decided to go to a local church fair. My son noticed it first, as we wondered along, he recognised all of the cars parked along the road and who they belonged to, "oh that's Barney's Mummy's car" and so on. It very quickly became obvious that in fact all the parent's cars from his class were parked along the road, perhaps they were going to the fair, I thought. Then I noticed balloons tied to William's front door, with Birthday emblazoned on them. All the children in the small cohort of 15 had been invited to the birthday party, with one notable exception. I would still like to know how you can try and reconcile this with a five-year-old and how you attempt to put them back together emotionally. It was very hurtful and served to cement my thoughts. Schools' suggestion to me, when I asked for advice, was to tell my child that not everyone can be invited to everything. This is true, but I live by the mantra of "small or all" it is never ok to leave just one child out.

As a child progresses further up the "food-chain" of academia, they may fall into significant depression. Often, they try and acquire friends by being the class clown and acting on their impulsive behaviour to gain attention and notoriety; this gives them the sense that they have status and self-respect. These juvenile attempts to increase their, "street-cred" usually end in disaster as they are typically too impulsive to think about the consequences of their actions before they do it and do not have the tools to verbalise the motivation for their behaviour afterwards. This leaves the ADHD child very vulnerable to exploitation and manipulation, be it from children who want to get them into trouble at school or for example gang culture outside of school, they will, eventually, do anything to feel included, wanted and accepted. We as humans all need to feel we belong—ADHD children are no different.

The above scenarios are all true for individuals who are not diagnosed. When left undiagnosed and untreated ADHD can decimate families and blight lives. If a child is diagnosed, this is extremely beneficial, for the whole family. You will become quickly aware throughout this book that the author is very pro-medication. The label that a diagnosis brings, not only serves as a tool to enable teachers and parents to understand the child better, but will also afford the individual reasonable adjustments, such as extra time in exams and quiet spaces to work or retreat to at playtime, access to counselling and medication, should it be so desired. However, medication is only part of the treatment for ADHD, it allows a child to have the brakes to be applied, so that they can learn to adhere to our social norms. Afterall society is not going

to change for the minority, even though it is a significant propor-
tion (20%) of the population, the minority must learn ways and
strategies to conform.

Subsequent sections of this book are intended as a practical guide
to help facilitate a smoother pathway for you and your child or
pupil.

# DIAGNOSIS

A class teacher, friend or family member, although they might have suspicions, is not qualified to say that your child has ADHD. Only a qualified clinician can diagnose, an opinion, however well meaning, is not a diagnosis.

Diagnosis of ADHD can be a long, time-consuming and potentially costly business. There are several routes open to families namely NHS (in the UK) or private. Both routes will involve a specialist paediatrician or clinical psychologist to conclude the diagnosis and may include an observation by a paediatric ADHD nurse. Both routes have their merits and their pitfalls, and will be discussed later. ADHD has to be diagnosed by clinicians as it caused by a neurotransmitter deficit of dopamine and noradrenaline in, predominantly the frontal lobe of the brain, and as such is considered a medical condition and not merely a learning disability.

In the UK for diagnosis to occur several criteria must be met, namely the child must be over six years old, symptoms must have been present or emerged before the age of twelve and symptoms must have been present in at least two or more settings for six months or longer.

I would urge anyone seeking a diagnosis to consider an assessment by an educational psychologist (EP) in addition to evaluation by a paediatrician. This serves to see if there are any other underlying co-existing conditions (co-morbidities) which may account for symptoms, such as dyslexia, dyspraxia etc. Even a good EP may not at this stage be able to identify all the underlying issues. This is not their fault. Consider it like layers of an onion, once a layer is peeled off (ADHD is managed) other symptoms e.g., persistent social impairment, as seen in ASD, (comorbidities) that may have been previously masked may start to emerge. An EP will be able to give a measure of the individual's underlying ability and therefore if they are achieving their potential or not. A good EP will then be able to point families towards professionals and services that may be able to help and advise on the next steps and interventions, including which strategies that school and home can both employ; a global approach towards the child's difficulties is always best.

## Before Diagnosis:

Parents and caregivers along with typically, but not exclusively, teachers will be asked to complete a series of questionnaires and forms detailing the developmental history of the child; these will go right back to gestation. Depending on which route you have decided to take, you will then wait for an appointment. Waiting during this time can cause all kinds of emotions, it can be torturous, you may well begin to doubt whether your child has any symptoms looking only for signs that your child is neurotypical or as it is now commonly referred to as non-neurodivergent. Alternatively, you may be very pragmatic and calm.

Whichever category you fit into, my best advice before the appointment, and in the weeks leading up is to make a plan, just as you would if you were bringing your new baby home from hospital for the first time. Plan ahead. Make some meals you can easily freeze ahead of time, things that are easy to reheat and that your family will eat. On the day or day before, if you have a morning appointment, make sure you have sorted the washing, and tidied the house so that it is one less thing for you to do on your return. If you feel you can, tell a trusted friend or family member about the appointment, you may want to talk to them afterwards or may need their support.

## Diagnosis—The Day Has Come

Reassure your child, that it will not be a nasty experience for them.

Even if you are quite sure about the diagnosis your child is about to receive, nothing will prepare you for how you might feel. It is perfectly normal to go through a whole range of emotions and this is quite understandable. It may also take some time for the news to sink in. You may feel denial, even if you were instrumental in initiating the appointments in the first place. You may feel relieved that someone is finally listening, or you might feel a mixed set of emotions. This is often a period of extreme stress and a grieving process for many families.

When you bring your child home afterwards remember they too have probably had a difficult day, be mindful to be kind to them, even if you are feeling upset yourself. Often doctors will discuss your child and their diagnosis in front of them, may not appear to understand or be listening. Likely as not they *are* listening, in part at least, and are quite possibly terrified. Make dinner something that you know they will eat, for this evening allow them to watch their favourite TV program and try and get them to bed in as normal a fashion as possible.

As much as you may have built this day up you may find that you emerge from the doctor's office having been told to return in six months, with no conclusive diagnosis. Remember what was written above, ADHD is a pervasive developmental disorder which has to be seen in two or more settings for at least six months or more.

At this stage you may have very strong feelings about medication, for or against, which I will discuss later, you may be disappointed that you have not got the prescription that you so desperately wanted. Or you may be relieved that medication has not been discussed. Over the next six months whichever camp you fall into, your opinion may change. If medication is mentioned at this stage and you are very against it, I urge you not to share this with the doctor. Rather adopt a wait and see approach. use different behavioural strategies that can be employed; you can always share your feelings, if you still feel this way, at a later date. There have been incidences of paediatricians "signing off" patients whose parents are violently opposed to medication, meaning that if they change their mind in the future, they may have to re-join the list and at the back of the queue.

This grieving process, is just that...a process and it will take the form of typical grief in its stages. If you are a teacher be mindful of this when you are talking to newly-diagnosed parents. They might be angry at you, in denial or very emotional. They will have to go through these stages before they can emerge, regroup and accept. It is counterproductive at this point to meet the parents with a barrage of their child's, obvious, failings; even if they have driven you crazy all day long. These parents are lost and love their child, but they are frightened – be kind. If you do choose to labour their child's short comings expect extreme hostility and a relationship that may be irreparably damaged.

It is my firm belief that children thrive best when they feel like both parents and teachers are working in harmony as a team try to foster good relationships between school and parents.

## After Diagnosis

Grief will pass and you will feel like you can get through this stressful period. Rely on friends and family to help you. If you can, reach out to support groups. As discussed above there may be a wait before medication can even be discussed. If strategies have been suggested, try them and see what works for your individual child. Spend the time educating yourself about ADHD – it will, after all, be with you for life. Discuss any findings from the doctor with the SENCO and class teacher and ask them to help you.

If you were like us, we emerged from the doctor's office with four (expected) letters slapped on my child and a leaflet; the rest was up to me—which is why I have written this book.

I think the most important thing to remember is that your child is still the same person you went into that room with. Whatever the driving force behind the visit was and whatever the outcome, your child is still yours and you love them. They need you, now more than ever, to continue to love and advocate for them. ADHD does not mean that your child will fail, have no friends, be lonely or jobless, it does mean that they and you will face extra challenges along the way. ADHD people with the right support have the same opportunities as the rest of the population, but with their, often, quirky take on the world they can see solutions to challenges that the general population cannot see.

## *The NHS Diagnosis:*

To follow this route, make an appointment with your G.P. and ask them to refer you for an ADHD assessment. It might be that they will require you to bring a letter from school or other outside source confirming that they also suspect ADHD so that they can initiate the referral process. Typically waiting lists are long (18-24 months).

The NHS is chronically short of community paediatricians, with more leaving the profession all the time and not enough joining. While they are very caring individuals, you may not see the same doctor regularly, if at all. They will do a thorough assessment of your child. However, they are not in control of the appointments, and although they may make recommendations to see your child within four months this can often be longer unless you call. A word of advice, when you receive your letter offering an appointment, there are often two numbers, one is the receptionist's number, the other is a direct line to the paediatric department. From experience you will get a faster appointment if you ring the paediatric department directly and relay symptoms and concerns. This will all be achieved with a telephone call but make sure you force yourself to smile, sound friendly and upbeat, they will be more helpful if you are nice!

The good news is that once you have a diagnosis, it will be accepted by school and other professional organisations, such as the LEA (local education authority). If you decide medication is the right course of action for your family then there will be a shared care agreement with your G.P. allowing them to provide you with repeat prescriptions.

## *The Private Diagnosis:*

This can be a costly route. Mental health conditions (which ADHD is considered to be due to the imbalance of neurotransmitters) may or may not be covered by private health insurance. The assessment procedure is the same for the NHS and is typically concluded within six months. Different doctors will charge different amounts, depending on which part of the country you are in, *i.e.,* the nearer London you are I would typically expect the price to increase. Naturally, the process differs in the fact that you may only have to wait as little as two weeks until you get your initial appointment.

It is very important to check with school or the LEA that any private diagnosis given is supported by them. If you decide on medication you will have to pay for private prescriptions, at least in the short term. This is an additional cost and it will vary depending on the type medication prescribed. Titration of the drugs will also be quicker, typically a practitioner will want to see you every two to four weeks initially (at a charge each time).

Once this is complete you may be able to enter into a shared care agreement with your G.P. allowing them to prescribe repeat prescriptions. However, your G.P. may not agree to such an arrangement, so be prepared if they are not, to withstand the costs. It is possible to be referred back into the NHS system, where the community paediatrics can take over the management after the initial diagnosis and titration is complete. In the meantime, before you can be added to the community paediatric NHS services you will have to be prepared to withstand the costs of any medication reviews and changes.

## *FAQ:*

Why bother with a diagnosis?

A diagnosis will provide protection, understanding and help for your child. As they progress through their education. Remember, every child is now required to be in full-time education until 18 years old. Demands and expectations from school will increase as your child gets older. A diagnosis, in the right institution, will alter expectations and afford reasonable adjustments for your child. These should be expected whether or not you choose medication. Do not be fobbed-off these are your child's legal rights.

What will a diagnosis achieve?

Apart from protection for your child and reasonable adjustments, you may be eligible to apply for DLA (disability living allowance) and carers allowance which will help with the additional costs of bringing up an ADHD child.

In the most basic terms, -a diagnosis will give you and your child a tangible understanding of and explanation for, their behaviour; and hopefully preserve both of you and your child's sanity when their ADHD symptoms might otherwise drive you mad! You might even laugh at some of their idiosyncrasies.

# MEDICATION, SUPPLEMENTS AND HOMEOPATHIC REMEDIES

I am not a paediatrician nor am I a physician, these are merely my thoughts as the mother of an ADHD child, along with my feelings and experiences and along with information that can be found in the general press.

**Always** seek medical advice before commencing with any medication or supplement.

The idea of medicating your child may be appalling to you, especially with controlled substances or "mind-altering" drugs. It might frighten you that you don't understand this medication or you may feel pressured by family and friends. You may have heard horror stories of medication turning children into zombies or causing them to be addicted. It might be that you are curious about medication, but know nothing about it. You might want to see if supplements and herbal medicine will be enough to help your child manage their symptoms. Alternatively, you may be pro-medication and want to start straight away. Whichever camp you fall into you owe it to yourself and your child to at least educate yourself on the available options to them.

It is best to make your decision about medication before sharing with family or friends, due to the polar positions people often take. Be prepared, whichever choice you make, for people to claim you are damaging your child. It is sadly a case of you are dammed if you do and dammed if you don't. I make no secret of the fact that I am extremely pro-medication, however, I do realise that it is a choice that is not for every family, for a variety of reasons and it is not my purpose to influence you either way.

Some ADHD medication (e.g., methyl phenidate) has been used for over fifty years and its effects and side-effects are well understood. If you choose medication, your practitioner will titrate your child with the relevant medication so that they use the lowest possible dose to achieve the maximum impact on managing symptoms (titration). For a very small number of cases medication is not effective or even an appropriate route, for example if there are pre-existing heart conditions or growth problems.

It is important to remember that medication is just one part of your tool kit and not a panacea. As children can only commence medication at around six years-old they may have already developed habits and inappropriate coping strategies for their ADHD, such as being the class clown or switching off. Medication should not be used as a stand-alone object and you will need to implement behaviour strategies to effect long term change. Medication, in my opinion, does give this the best chance of success. ADHD children are neurodivergent, meaning that they have atypical brain chemistry, medication goes some way to redressing the chemical imbalance within their brains. It is a case of winning the battle, the war is yet to be won.

## *Titration*

Titration takes time, there is no blood test available to see if symptoms have dissipated, this can only be done by close observation of caregivers and school. Medication is initially given in low doses of immediate release preparations. Typically, the short acting doses last between 3-5 hours, meaning that if side effects are severe or intolerable the medication can be terminated with no long-lasting or residual effects. This is to see if the child can tolerate the drugs and to observe the impact on symptoms.

Slowly, if needed, the strength and type of preparation (usually sustained release) will be changed, until symptoms are minimised. This can take some considerable time, with medication strength being increased in small increments every 2-4 weeks or sometimes months. During this phase parents and school need to monitor the child carefully to see if symptom control is adequate and that side effects are tolerable.

Once titration is complete your child will be reviewed every six months to see if blood pressure, growth and weight are progressing normally and that symptoms remain under control. You and school will be asked to complete ADHD rating scales questionnaires, to see if the current dose is appropriate or if it needs changing. This is a constant feedback loop for parents and school. Be mindful and carefully observe for the re-emergence of symptoms before you fill in the questionnaires, as this may be the only opportunity you have for the next six months to speak to your paediatrician.

A word about tablets. The majority of ADHD medication is taken in pill form. Sustained release preparations, such as Concerta XL, must not be crushed or chewed, therefore you will need to teach your child to swallow tablets. The easiest way of doing this is practise, obviously it would not be appropriate to use real medicine, we used Tic-Tacs and a large glass of water until our child was able to reliably swallow even the largest of pills without issues.

## Side Effects

Do not be put off by these, as with all medications the clinical benefit to the individual must be outweighed by the costs of not having medication and the side effects. All drugs, however natural (think of cocaine), have side effects. Manufactures have to list all side effects even if they are extremely rare, if you are at all concerned discuss candidly with your clinician who will advise and support your decision-making process.

There is a long list of side effects associated with ADHD medications. It is very likely that your child will experience some of these to varying degrees. It is important to remember that the majority of these are transient and will settle down after a short time.

Remember that you will need to be compassionate towards your child as they experience them. Try and make life as easy and as comfortable as you can. Don't be confrontational they are highly likely to be feeling a whole raft of emotions.

My child has likened medication to seeing the world in clarity for the first time, as if a veil had been removed from in front of his eyes. This new and heightened reality might not be particularly palatable. It might make them realise they are not as popular with their cohort, teachers and siblings as they thought and it might be very distressing for them. They may suddenly realise that they are not achieving academically as well as they thought they were. All this leads to a plummet in their self-esteem and you will need to be there to reassure them and make them feel they are not alone. Make accommodations for them if they find their appetite is altered, they may ask for something to eat and then leave the food untouched, do not get angry but continue to offer small amounts of high value food frequently. Some side effects can be useful, for example the somnolence associated with the non-stimulant medication Intuniv allowed my child to sleep for the night. This was the first time my son had managed this in his entire 8 years—we both felt better! This side effect has, sadly, since worn off, but it still helps!

## *The Cinderella Effect.*

When my child first started medication, he was 5 years and 10 months. The results were phenomenal. He could suddenly follow instructions, eat a meal with the rest of the family without darting out of the room. He could get dressed independently, was cooperative, and for him it was truly amazing—he was finally at peace. However, at 3:45 every afternoon the medication clearly wore off, and not slowly, rapidly. Within five minutes you could see all the symptoms emerging like The Hulk transforming into himself, or like Cinderella suddenly back in her rags, surrounded by mice and a pumpkin. I was devasted for him. He went form a calm and quiet child, whom you could describe as having inner peace to a tortured soul pulling his socks off with his teeth, unable to function as he had but thirty minutes previously. I had a glimpse each day of how wonderful my child could be; less driven, rested and mentally at peace, which was wonderful and then the monster exerted his power and took my gorgeous child from me and left him exhausted. This can be improved by altering types and timings of doses, e.g., sustained release preparations which give better coverage throughout the day, but as ever this has to be monitored carefully.

To compound the problem titration was made more difficult as my child is a fast metaboliser—meaning the duration of the effects of medication were shortened significantly. As a result, we have had the Cinderella effect happen many times and we have tried the majority of the medication I am about to discuss. We often assess our child to see if "Jack is coming out of the box." For the moment we seem to have reached some stability; his current medication, he has been taking for 18 months and it feels like it is working—for now!

## Stimulants

It seems perverse that a seemingly overstimulated and hyperactive child needs a stimulant, such as amphetamine, to calm them down, but the mechanism of action of these drugs increases the amount of dopamine and norephedrine (noradrenaline) available to the brain and thus redresses the neurochemical balance.

Methyl phenidate and dextroamphetamine are stimulants and are often the first choice and most commonly prescribed medications for ADHD. They have been in use since the late 1940's and come in a variety of immediate and sustained release preparations. They include Medikinet XL, Concerta, Elvance, Vyance and Ritalin to name but a few.

Mechanism of action: This class of drug is called central nervous system (CNS) stimulant medication. They work by increasing the amounts of the neurotransmitters dopamine and norephedrine (noradrenaline) in the brain.

Common Side effects:

Weight loss, appetite suppression, insomnia, developmental growth delays, stomach ache, headache, dysphoria (complete absence of pleasure or joy), tics (involuntary movements or vocalizations), anxiety, confusion, irritability, withdrawal, psychosis (highly unusual beliefs, hallucinations).

## *Non-Stimulants*

Non-stimulants take longer to take effect, typically 6 weeks, however they may be taken in conjunction with a stimulant medication. It is important to know that these drugs cannot just be stopped the individual must slowly wean themselves off the medication to mitigate against high blood pressure, in the case of Intuniv. Therefore, the compliance of the individual taking the medication is essential.

Mechanism of actions: These drugs also affect neurotransmitters, but they don't increase dopamine levels.

They are usually prescribed when stimulants cannot be given, e.g., if side effects are intolerable, or are ineffective; sometimes they are prescribed in conjunction with stimulant medication.

Strattera allows norepinephrine work longer in the brain. The drug is long-acting, it is taken it once per day – often increasing compliance in teenagers.

Side effects: Sleep problems, anxiety, somnolence, upset stomach, dizziness, dry mouth. Although rare, can cause liver damage. Higher risk of suicide in adults aged 18-24.

Intuniv was initially prescribed for high blood pressure in adults, however it was discovered to have a potent effect in the treatment of ADHD. This drug is approved for use in children with ADHD. It may help with memory and behavioural problems and can improve aggression and hyperactivity.

Common side effects: somnolence, dizziness, dry mouth, irritability, behaviour problems, low blood pressure. Stopping this medicine suddenly can result in high blood pressure.

## Melatonin

Also known as the sleep hormone, can be bought over the counter in Europe and the USA, but not currently in UK. It is the hormone, produced naturally by humans, responsible for circadian rhythm, that tells us when it is time to start feeling sleepy and is often used by frequent travellers to alleviate the problems associated with jet lag. It can be prescribed for persistent sleep issues to children with ADHD, and can be helpful, although its efficacy long-term is questionable.

## Omega 3 & 6

There is substantial evidence to support the benefits of taking omega 3 & 6 oils for children and adults with a multitude of impairments, including dyslexia, eye problems, dyspraxia, autism, ODD, PDA the list goes on.[4] There is a link between improved cognitive function and omega 3 and 6 fatty acids. It has been suggested in the literature that they can be a good supplement or alternative to (for those who cannot tolerate) stimulant medication. It is certainly worthwhile exploring this avenue and discussing with the relevant professionals.

## L-Theanine

L-Theanine is an amino acid that is able to cross the blood brain barrier, a fatty sheath that surrounds and protects the brain—only specific chemicals are able to pass through. It affects the brain by increasing the levels of serotonin and dopamine neurotransmitters, thus alleviating the ADHD symptoms.[5]

## 5-HTP

5-HTP is an amino acid, and is the immediate precursor to the neurotransmitter serotonin it passes readily through the blood brain barrier. Serotonin is responsible for the regulation of sleep, appetite and mood. There is some evidence that this is a useful supplement to alleviate ADHD symptoms.[5]

## Magnesium

Biological systems use magnesium to transmit messages along their nervous systems. In addition, it promotes relaxation in the muscles. There is evidence to suggest that ADHD children are deficient in magnesium.[5]

## Zinc

Zinc can contribute to behavioural changes through its regulatory effects on certain brain neurotransmitters, melatonin and fatty acids.[5]

# SLEEP

It cannot be overstated enough; how important sleep is for a whole family. If anyone has seen any new parents recently, they will see first-hand what the effects of sleep deprivation are, seemingly intelligent people become mere shells of their former selves unable to do the most mundane tasks due to their lack of sleep. Fortunately, for most people, this intense period of tiredness is transient. This is true, unless you are the parent of an ADHD child, sleep deprivation continues on well beyond that of their peer group and can leave both parents and child feeling perpetually exhausted. Most ADHD children do not get enough sleep. This section will encompass some methods for behaviour change, which will be dealt with more thoroughly in later chapters.

However, the focus here is sleep, once this can be remediated the whole family will feel its benefit and be able to function more efficiently which will allow other more effective behaviour changes to take place. As with so many things it is important to remember that all parenting styles differ and can even vary wildly within families. It is essential that any approach used is consistent and that all adults involved are in agreement for the best possible chances of success.

ADHD is not merely a problem that eliminates at night time when children sleep. Three quarters of children with ADHD suffer with sleep problems.[6] Children can be anxious and resistant about bed time. They can have difficulty falling asleep, maintaining sleep, and waking up in the morning. Alternatively, they may be very early risers or be unable to fall back to sleep on their own once they have woken up. Movement during their sleep is often significantly higher than their non-neurodivergent counterparts.

Noise, of any kind, in the night can cause them to wake, I used to say even a snail slithering across my child's floor would awaken him. He would often look like a panda with huge dark rings around his eyes, despite having apparently had 6-8 hours sleep, which is not enough for a four-year-old!

The challenges that ADHD people face during the day can lead them to be more tired than an average child. It would seem cruelly perverse then that they have such trouble in getting the sleep that they so desperately need. I will detail here some strategies I have found most effective in helping alleviate sleep problems for the whole family.

## Light

Many children like to have a night light as a source of comfort in their bedrooms at night. There are fashionable clocks available on the market that show a child it is night and when it is day time *via* colour changing, sadly these clocks often display blue light to indicate it is night time. I am not a fan of any blue light in bedrooms, as this has been shown to disturb melatonin production, the sleep-inducing hormone.

Perhaps it is more important to consider when we want a child to sleep, especially an ADHD child, the light that they are exposed to up to three hours before sleep actually needs to happen. The time you want your child to sleep will, inevitably, be well before your child's feet reach the bottom of the stairs in preparation for bed. To set the scene for good sleep, set the mood by having soft lighting that is not from LED bulbs or overhead lights. Keep the light level dim, but not so dim that you cannot see; imagine the tone as if you were trying to create a romantic atmosphere—where you and your child's love affair with sleep can begin! When you go upstairs, again have a soft light instead of a well-lit landing, draw the curtains (and blind) in the bedroom and immediately switch the night light on and maybe a targeted reading light—but turn the overhead lights off.

Which night light to choose? We have been through several over the years. The best, and least expensive, by far have been Himalayan salt lamps. They provide a soft pink glow, and you can easily replace the bulbs with dimmer ones if you need to. They are safe to be left on all night, and allegedly help promote sleep.

Some ADHD children need noise to fall asleep, we have explored this option too, you can purchase lights with water and plastic fish in, they change colour and make a white noise, while blowing bubbles through the water inside. They are not cheap and I would advise caution before investing. On some of these lights, the tops are not secure, so when they are knocked over, the contents are spilt over the floor, leaving an unholy mess. In addition, the change in colour, although predictable, can in my experience excite some children, leaving them to want to do anything but sleep.

A word about curtains and blinds. When our ADHD-er was little we invested in both blackout blinds and blackout curtains, particularly useful in summer. Any chink of light when he woke at night was enough to be the death knell to anymore sleep. Summer is a difficult time, for all of us, to get enough quality sleep it is something that a routine can help with.

## Noise

As I mentioned earlier, I used to joke a snail slithering across the floor was enough to awaken my child or indeed keep him awake. He can still tell me what time the milkman delivers milk to the neighbours; and if he is late doing his rounds! Try and keep noise normal, by this I mean you can never eliminate noise completely, heating systems will go on and off, baths and showers will be used and so on. However, if noises are predictable, they will soon assimilate themselves into the normal routine and will cease to be a distraction for your child.

Make sure that you bleed radiators before you turn on the central heating in autumn. Plan to start the heating to go on during the first weekend of half term. This is so that any unfamiliar noises from the heating will become, hopefully, white noise over the course of the week and they won't be going to school, where they have to concentrate, tired. If you have a load of washing to do most evenings, run the machine at the time you have just left your child's room, the rhythmic cycle and predictable end can be comforting for a child.

Not all noise can be eliminated. People will need the toilet, have to make phone calls etc, but try where you can to make the noise as predictable as possible.

Some children find it easier to drift off to sound. There are devices you can buy which will play stories or music. I would steer away from anything that requires a response, as this will end up as stimulation and sleep will be the last thing on the child's mind. We found playing soft jazz music helpful, and it is something that will grow with our child, after all, who wants to be 12 and caught out listening to 'My Naughty Little Sister' on audio book, even if it is comforting for them. Whatever you choose make sure that it is predictable and not stimulating.

## Temperature

Too hot, too cold. One of the side effects of stimulant medication is that it can make children very sensitive to heat. If your child is anything like mine, they will detest being hot. It can be very difficult in summer.

Have cotton sheets, they allow for skin to breathe and whip away sweat. Swap in summer to old fashioned sheets and blankets rather than just a duvet all year round. If you use a weighted blanket (they can be very useful) consider switching to a t-shirt material that wraps around the bed. Keep the room well ventilated. You could consider having a tower fan, which will provide white noise (if your child likes this), but have it set in one direction rather than sweeping across the room—too much distraction otherwise.

Perversely, although my child is a heat sufferer, he loves to have a hot water bottle in winter, the rhythmic sloshing sounds that it makes are comforting, I often fill it with ice cold water in summer. When it is very hot, we tend to run a tepid bath, half full, immerse the children and then turn on the cold tap, until they are thoroughly chilled. This allows them enough time to nod off while still feeling cool.

## Bed Clothes

Pick cotton, or high percentage cotton clothes. Your child may not like the feeling of bed clothes and although there may be a draw full of expensive nightwear available to them it really shouldn't matter if they sleep with nothing on at all. Your child may find clothing constricting or that seams and labels are too much to bear against their skin, if this is the case there are specialist suppliers who manufacture items which are seamless, however they are expensive. Try removing labels from clothes first if this is the issue.

Conversely, your child may find it calming and soothing to stroke the satin label on their clothing. It is then quite easy to acquire a piece of satin cloth, or several pieces for them to stroke or suck as they drift off, much easier and more comfortable than contorting a body to get into the right position for that perfect sensory moment.

## Bed Linen

As said earlier, make it cotton, that way it will allow skin to breathe and absorb any sweat keeping your child more comfortable. Make it plain, that way it can grow with your child—imagine the embarrassment of being 16 and still having Thomas the Tank Engine bedding just because it feels perfect for you!

In summer opt for cotton flat and fitted sheets, layers can then be peeled off according to temperature and hospital corners can be employed if having compression is desired without getting too hot.

## Electronics

There should be **NO** electronic items other than night light and possibly an audio system (that you control) in your child's bedroom. This includes, for older children tablets, phones and electronic games consoles. For younger children anything that contains batteries should also be removed.

Moreover, it is a good idea to turn off the T.V. about two hours before the main event, along with phones, tablets etc. The blue light that they emit is not sleeps friend.

## Toys

The majority of children's toys should be in a room used most by the family. Afterall none of us chose to have children to put them in their bedrooms the whole time; they are not toys and don't need to be, "put away". Books and maybe a few quiet toys for young children in their rooms are fine if they are really struggling. The message that you are trying to deliver, loud and clear, is that this is a room for one purpose, and one only, and that is sleeping.

### *Bedroom Layout*

Check in with your child, is their room the way they want it to be? When we moved house I spent a long time unpacking and arranging the children's rooms. It was only a few months later that my child said to me that the arrangement was not really what he would like. The position of the bed was all wrong, so we changed it and he was much happier.

### *Routine*

Routines may seem very regimented, but the ADHD child desperately needs this structure, it will provide comfort, predictability and cues to help them go to sleep.

The importance of a routine cannot be overstated or reiterated enough. ADHD kids are, typically, very disorganised. It is helpful to check their school bags for right equipment each evening and as they get older, put up a weekly list of what to check each night for themselves. This way the morning will be a lot less stressful too and hopefully will get them into good habits as they get older.

All humans thrive on routine, it allows us to predictably know what is coming next and will send cues to our brains. The predictability of a routine also provides comfort. Parents of small children should be solely in charge, as a child grows allow them to adapt and add to the routine, this way they will more likely adhere to it and it will become a firm foundation for life.

I find it best to stick to a bath every night; bathing can be a very relaxing experience. Do not have too many bath toys or sensory items in the bath, this is supposed to be a winding down period. Do use essential oils and other relaxing bath washes etc to help your child relax. Stay with them while they are in the bath and talk to them. This allows them to engage with you, they may tell you more about their day at this stage as they start to wind down. Remind your child about what will be coming next. Brush their teeth, or at least supervise; sounds silly I know, but ADHD children are typically more immature than their years. Supervised brushing and washing will need to occur for much longer than you would have expected at the time of their birth. Discuss the importance of personal hygiene; if you say it long enough, they might actually remember it when they're teenagers!

Read a story. Pick a book that is in a reading age bracket above their reading level, this can serve to be more interesting and will expose them to vocabulary that they have not yet encountered in their own reading. Discuss the book, again sounds silly, but see if they can predict what will come next and if they have truly understood the inference in the text. It is important to remember there is a cross-over of symptoms between ADHD and ASD, inference is one of the things that is essential in reading at higher levels and something that ASD people struggle with. Ask your child if they can remember prior events in the text, this will help them engage more with the story and improve memory skills.

Make sure you leave enough time to have a chat one-to-one, tell them about your day and find out about theirs—even for a much older child. This might be the time they decide to unload a bomb-shell of a difficult day onto you. If this is the case it is a good thing that they feel secure enough to share it with you, although their timing might be better! Do your best to comfort them in this scenario and work out an action plan, tell them you are in it together, this way they are not taking their problems into a sleepless night and they don't feel alone.

Try, where possible, to have the same adult follow the routine in the beginning. Although you and your partner may be singing from the same hymn sheet, inevitably you will have different styles. Have a day off too, e.g., Saturday, where your partner can take the reins and give you chance to relax; this way the child will feel like they are getting a reward as it will be different and thus a treat and this might come in handy if you need to use Achilles' heel—see below!

Whatever you decide on make sure it is maintainable and manageable for your family. There is little point exhausting yourself in pursuit of a routine that is unachievable, all that will happen is that you give up, get angry or end up in an asylum—none of which is productive.

A routine with your child and children should be one you can both agree on and achieve together, this means that all parties must buy into the process.

## *Achilles Heel*

This may seem harsh, but there will come a day when your child will live independently, they will need to have a sleep routine deeply rooted within them—or they might really struggle in the adult world!

Almost certainly there will be some resistance in the initial stages of the process of implementing a new routine, even if it has been agreed upon. That does not mean that it won't work, it means it will take time, be patient.

ADHD children work on immediate rewards and consequence. Star charts at bed time are, from my experience, ineffective and can even be detrimental. Stars maybe awarded throughout the day for good behaviour and then, through anger or frustration, are removed at bedtime when everyone is tired and has had enough.

Bedtime should be non-negotiable, even if they are not able to sleep themselves, out of consideration for others in the home they must remain quiet and in their room; this is particularly true if children have to share bedrooms.

The old adage that, "mother knows best," is true here; you know your child better than anyone else. You will also be acutely aware what they enjoy and value most in the world, *i.e.*, their Achilles Heel! Use this to your advantage, but do not abuse it. Agree with your child before-hand the sanction that will be imposed if they break the rule, so that they are aware. Expect World War Three for a few nights. They will test the boundary and you will have to deploy the Achilles Heel; they will be very angry, upset and distraught, but you must follow through. If you need to, you can use a sliding scale of sanctions. Make sure this is a sanction that you are prepared to execute, there is very little point banning something for a week if you are unable to follow through; and a week can feel like an eternity to a small child—and you! Make the punishment fit the crime.

The best sanctions are those you will be able to implement every day, and shortly after misdemeanour or immediately the following day. Sanctions are not effective if they are implemented days after the event. For example, if the sanction is no T.V. your child will awaken the following morning, having broken the rules the previous night, and quite possibly will have chosen to forget you telling them there would be no T.V. that day. Expect a battle when they realise you are maintaining your stance. This will be really effective if you keep your cool. Don't enter into an argument with them but remind them of the rule and the sanction that you both agreed would take place. This technique is even more effective if there are other children in the home, who will naturally not be punished, unless of course they also broke the rules too. Make it fair, so the focus child doesn't feel victimised, if another child breaks the rule, then they too must be sanctioned. Very quickly your child will get the message. Don't offer a reward at the same time the sanction is being imposed, no T.V. does not mean making a cake with you, eating chocolate or other fun 1:1 time, it needs to feel painful, but you need to be calm and resolute. Do not engage in warfare, it will only escalate the situation and you may cave in, have a matter-of-fact tone and tell your child they will have another opportunity to make the right choice that evening.

Alternative activities should be productive but not a reward, such as reading a book, doing a puzzle, helping you with an errand or a task.

## Buying Into the Process

Discipline techniques have the best chance of success if you can get your child to feel involved in the whole process, particularly if your child is older. Start by explaining to them the importance of sleep and how tired they and you are. Explain that you are not being the best you can be and you know that life will feel better if you can all get more rest.

Listen carefully to your child, ask if there is anything that they would like you to do to help them sleep better; it might be something that you used to do when they were much smaller and have abandoned because it seemed too babyish. Indulge them where possible, such as for an older child a bedtime story. This has to be on the understanding that bedtime is just that, and there will be no rewards. Bedtime is not a reason for a reward, it is an expectation to be quiet, at least if they can't sleep, they must not disturb others from getting rest.

## *Non-Medication Interventions to Help Sleep*

There are some non-prescribed options available which help to encourage sleep. How effective they are is debatable, however even if they have the placebo effect, they have served their purpose. One such option is Montmorency Cherry juice which proports to be a natural source of melatonin. It is quite tart but palatable and can be found in health food shops. Another, which is fairly new to the market, is a flavoured milk with added supplements like valerian. The milk is very thick and the flavour is reasonable, however it is very expensive.

How much sleep does a child need?

*Taken from the NHS website 2020.*

- **6** **years**--night-time: 10 hours 45 minutes
- **7** **years**--night-time: 10 hours 30 minutes
- **8** **years**--night-time: 10 hours 15 minutes
- **9** **years**--night-time: 10 hours
- **10** **years**--night-time: 9 hours 45 minutes
- **11** **years**--night-time: 9 hours 30 minutes
- **12** **years**--night-time: 9 hours 15 minutes
- **13** **years** --night-time: 9 hours 15 minutes
- **14** **years**--night-time: 9 hours
- **15** **years**--night-time: 9 hours
- **16** **years**--night-time: 9 hours

*FAQ:*

My child is a, "Jack-in-the-Box," what do I do?

Deliver them back to bed, remind them of the rule and the sanction once, then impose the sanction.

My child doesn't seem to care about the sanction the following day, what do I do?

You need to find their Achilles heel! Even if it hurts you in the short term.

My child wakes too early?

Remind them of the rule once after that follow it with the sanction, if they are disturbing others. Allow them to read or look at some books quietly if they really can't return to sleep; praise them in front of other family members for doing the right thing or making the right choice if they do. Do not offer a reward other than verbal praise. If they are persistently waking up too early consider a later bedtime.

Nothing is working, we are *so* tired!

Stick with it, routines can take a long time to adjust to, this is a battle in a war! Examine the routine see if there are areas for flexibility. It might be there are other issues that your child is not able to verbalise. They might be being bullied, or feeling low about themselves. It might be that you bring them into bed with parents in the short term for comfort, or allow them to fall asleep in the parental bed on the understanding that they return to their own room when you go to sleep. It will be a transient phase, but it will make them feel more secure and nurtured. Let them know that you are on their side and that you are in this together, that way they will not feel alone.

## *Sample routine*

Here is how we do it. It takes about two hours, but then I have three children with age ranges from 20 months to 10 years. I will refer to them as 1, 2 and 3 (with 3 being the littlest). This is a very simple routine that works well, although it is time consuming. Having and ADHD child in the house might make you think that life is going faster, in reality everything can take much longer. If you can manage a sleep routine that works for you and your family life will get a lot less tricky and you will all feel its positive effects. Develop a routine that works for you and your family.

5 pm dinner – everyone eats together and talks at the kitchen table. There is no T.V. no radio and no phones at mealtime.

5:30 1 & 2 help clear away and put the dirty things in the sink not everyone has a table

5:35 we all watch T.V. together

6:00 we all go upstairs for a bath, 2&3 together and then 1 separately while I am getting 3 into nightclothes. I bob in to remind to wash body and hair. Medication is taken and I clean/supervise cleaning teeth (1-3)—note ADHD children are typically 3-5 years more immature than their years so I make sure teeth are cleaned properly.

6:30 3 and often 2 will have a story together, while 1 is getting dry.

6:40 3 to bed

6:40-7:15 1&2 in their own rooms with book, wordsearch, crossword, simple (independent maths game). The aim of this is that it allows me to go and load the dishwasher, more importantly it allows them to have some time on their own away from any kind of external stimulus. They are given tasks to do, which they know I will expect them to have attempted on my return. They also know there will be consequences if they make noise or come out of their bedrooms at this time.

7:15 check in on 1-deliver, hot water bottle. Check 2 has done task, ask about inference and comprehension of reading material, check understanding of maths. Play a quick, educationally relevant, game (I will discuss these in a later chapter). Read story, the choice of story is beyond reading age, as this exposes him to vocabulary that he might not encounter. Then bed.

7:35 Repeat for 1 (ADHD-child) as above. When the light is out remind about the behaviour that is expected, not what is not expected. For example, "I'm going to have a bath now, it's bed time and I expect you to stay in bed with your reading light off". Not "I'm going to have a bath now; you're not going to come out of your bed, are you?". I find it's very important what language you use; try not to sow the seeds of ideas you do not wish to happen. Note this is when all things are plain sailing, there are times when events have occurred that the situation will be different, but this is our typical evening. If events have occurred, that have unsettled or upset your child, be flexible, be kind and give them that extra time to unpack their day. This is their special 1:1 time with you and you might be the only person they feel secure enough to share with. More about this in later chapters.

# DISCIPLINE AND BEHAVIOURAL CHANGES

Discipline does not mean the same as punishment and it is essential for the ADHD child to thrive. Discipline means to train a person to be able to control themselves, while medication helps, it is not a stand-alone object and will not remediate behaviour on its own. There is a phrase used with regard to medication "once you can reach them you can teach them", this means that once there is medication in effect, they will be more receptive towards behaviour changes because they will be able to apply the brakes of thinking time. Discipline must, of course, be imposed from an outside source, namely the parents, before it can be imposed by the individual themselves.

ADHD people are typically immature compared to their non-neurodivergent peers by between three and five years, this means that a 10-year-old might behave more like a five-year-old and therefore the disciplinary techniques imposed must be appropriate for their adjusted age group. These differences can be seen well into adulthood; however, the good news is the gap does narrow as they get older. This difference also leaves ADHD children significantly more vulnerable to manipulation and it is perhaps more important to influence their behaviour at a young age and get them into good routines that will hopefully stand them in good stead for the rest of their lives.

Behaviour change is not a quick fix, it takes time, patience, understanding and a good deal of good humour, along with the all-important consistency. Don't lose sight of why you are doing this in the first place, namely that you are preparing your child for the adult world and so that they can make appropriate life choices that will be positive. There is a saying "give me a child until he is seven and I will have him for life," the good news is that you may have your seven-year-old like child for a bit longer, more likely when he is ten or twelve years old because of the lag in their brain development and therefore their behaviour.

It is highly likely that your child will be extremely resistant to discipline changes in the first instance; stick with your long-term plan-be resolute but also have compassion.

## *How and when to effect change*

Find a relative period of calm in your child's life. There is little point adding stress and pressure to an already tumultuous system at its peak. Do not try an effect significant changes if your child has just started medication, or has school tests or exams etc allow side effects to dissipate and then commence with your action plan.

Choose one or two behaviours at a time to change. Rome was not built in a day and your child will not change their behaviour overnight. I would suggest bedtime to be a great place to start, once you and your child feel better rested you will be more able to cope with any demanding behaviour and they will be more receptive towards discipline when they know you mean business.

Be explicit about the behaviours you want to change and let your child know with honesty. Give them an explanation why these changes have to happen; if they can understand the reasons for you wanting them and things to change, they are more likely to adhere to the new regime with less resistance. Explain what will happen if you see them repeating the behaviour *i.e.*, the consequence. Make sure you are able and willing to follow through. I would expect you to have to implement consequences a good number of times before you see real changes. When you have to initiate a consequence do it in as emotionless state as you can, use the phrase "you know the rules and next time you will make a different choice". Expect extreme resistance, argument and amateur dramatics! A child in the cold light of day will promise you many, many, things that in the heat of the moment are forgotten. This is why it is important to only choose one or two behaviours at a time; choose too many and it will fail, as will weakening and not following through with a consequence. When you catch your child doing the right thing make a point of noticing it and praise them often and publicly. All children want to please the adults around them so feed the good behaviour with adulation.

Consequence and praise need to be consistent and meted out in the moment, there is no point chastising or punishing an ADHD child for something that happened over an hour ago. ADHD children live in the moment and when that moment has passed, they do not reflect on their own actions readily.

## Pick your Battles

When you have decided on a behaviour to change stick with it! There may be many annoying or irritating things your child does, but unless its life threatening or dangerous do not call them out or nag. They can be addressed at a later date. Stick with the focus behaviours and try and turn a blind eye—give yourself a time out, count to ten, whatever works but don't nag; you will only become "wallpaper" and will cease to have any impact on their behaviour.

Never ever get into an argument with your ADHD child; they are the masters at arguments and thrive on them. They will always seek to have the last word and draw you into further argument. Feel confident that you are the adult in charge and ultimately have overall control—in the words of Elsa, 'Let it go'!

## Achilles Heel

To really effect changes in your child's behaviour you will need to find their Achilles Heel. This could be a treasured object, although it should never be a favourite e.g., teddy they have at bedtime. However, if your child likes to carry their teddy in the car or to school you can enforce imprisonment of the precious object in the bedroom, where it will only be returned for sleep. The best Achilles Heels are those that other children in the household enjoy too, such as a tablet, a club, the T.V., something that they may have to watch the other child enjoying while they are serving their time. Be fair and have consequences for siblings too and make sure that they have them imposed so the focus child doesn't feel victimised.

Have an agreed consequence for misbehaviour before a misdemeanour occurs. Regardless of your frustration don't change the goal posts by enhancing the consequence or extending the length of time it is to be levied. Don't, during the time of consequence, offer a more attractive alternative, for example a games console instead of the tablet, the consequence has to hurt. Be matter of fact when imposing the consequence with the phrase that you knew the rule and hopefully next time your child will make a better choice.

Offer a choice of activity that is quiet and you know they will do as an alternative. It might be that you will have to sit with them while they do this. It would be beneficial to the child to non-judgementally reflect on the event and how a different outcome could have been achieved. This can work really effectively if you can draw on some of your own misdemeanours from the past so you can model to the child how you recovered from mistakes. Always remind the child that you love them but not the problem behaviour.

## Rewards and Reinforcement

I find star charts and marbles in a jar to be ineffective, I forget to add them in and in the heat of the moment I am sorely tempted to remove them. A far better approach is to run two schemes simultaneously, which I call, Rewards and Reinforcement.

It works like this: Using the Achilles Heel as a consequence is part of the reinforcement system, something or time on something is removed. Rewards are where you give your child something, but here is the catch; they have to earn it. It could be you choose one behaviour, a more serious one, for reinforcement and a less tricky behaviour for rewards.

For rewards I use money, hard cash in 5 penny pieces in a jam-jar up to £2, although the monetary values can be altered to make the end amount appropriate for the age of the child. The amount given should not be too high, you don't want them to be able to afford a video game only to have to remove it that afternoon *via* the Achilles Heel. I award the money to my children; both have the same technique imposed I find it works best. (only one of my children has ADHD) Then I tell them that all this lovely money is theirs to keep, (their little faces are painted with delight and avarice akin to King Midas by this stage), and can be spent on whatever they choose. However, and here is the caveat; the money is only theirs at the end of the week, if they adhere to the chosen behaviour, with a fine imposed each time they flout the rule. Every time you see the problem behaviour impose the fine; let them know that you spotted the behaviour and what you are doing but don't be confrontational. Initially, the child may not think it's not too bad, because they still have plenty of cash still left in their jar, however this will soon run out. You are aiming week one, for the fines to be sufficient that little or no money remains by the end of the week; make sure you fine the siblings too and that they will also receive virtually nothing by day 7. At the end of the week, reflect with your child in as non-judgemental a way as possible, on the week's events, before you bring out the money. Ask them how they think they did, then count out the cash in a matter-of-fact way. Be cheerful, tell them that next week you know they will do better and receive more money. Explain to them because you are so sure of this the value of the money in the jar will remain the same but the fine will go up—this is why you choose this technique for the less tricky behaviour as it's more achievable. Expressly tell them how pleased you are and that you did notice them sticking to the rule several times and that you are confident they can achieve this end goal. Once you have that particular desired behaviour dealt with you can introduce a new behaviour to work on. I find this is the fastest way to achieve behaviour change.

It maybe that a change is transient only for the problem behaviour to re-emerge after a few weeks, it is a good idea to revisit past behaviours for a reminder every now and then.

## Hard rules and soft rules

Some rules at home and in society are "hard" rules, *i.e.*, rules which should never be broken. Some are "soft" rules, which carry a consequence if broken, but are not as serious.

Hurting, stealing, vandalism, lying, bullying are all hard rules, they are not acceptable under any circumstance and should rightly result in exclusion until the child has calmed down and you are able to discuss with them quietly what happened. Do not attempt to approach them until they are calm, they will not listen and you might inflame the situation further. Send them to a quiet spot, or remove yourself and siblings.

Soft rules are behaviours that reflect social norms and customs, such as sitting down to eat dinner, not taking your brother's toy without asking etc.

If you have a hard rule breaker, life can be very tough. You will need to impose hard consequences. Be mindful to be compassionate. Children are not born bad, there may be an underlying reason for their behaviours. This could include bullying others at school, impulsivity, hitting as a result of frustration, manipulation by the peer group and low self-esteem. ADHD means that a child will be impulsive and do things without considering the consequences but it does not mean that the child is wilfully malicious or unkind. There is almost always a reason behind this type of behaviour and you may need to really help the overwhelmed ADHD child vocalise their thoughts, which will undoubtedly be jumbled, so that they can calmly tell you what the root cause is. You will still need to explain explicitly why the behaviour is not acceptable. You must still impose a consequence for this behaviour, although it is highly likely your child will be accepting of this once they understand why you or their teacher is upset and they have had some time to calm down. Remember in the grown-up world there is a hard consequence for such behaviours, called prison, which will have far reaching effects on your child's life. It is worth pointing this out to your child if it is a persistent problem.

## Social skills, matching your behaviour and weird thoughts.

Fidgety, fiddly fingers, curiosity, noisy, talking incessantly, poor impulse control, running as if driven by a motor, chronically exhausted; the ADHD child crashes through life. Annoying, aggravating and infuriating those around them, both children and adults alike. I used to say my child never entered a room he arrived like a tornado over the threshold, in a jumble of detritus that he would scatter in his wake. Like a puppy sitting next to a pile of fresh poo he would have the best of motives and intentions but couldn't see how he had ended up yet another situation and was, and still is always, deeply apologetic.

Explicit and repeated gentle teaching about an ADHD child's social faux pas is the only method of intervention that will remediate the situation. There are some general rules of thumb but they will need to be adapted for your unique child. Do not use a consequence or the Achilles heel for this. The rejection and ridicule meted out by your child's peer group and eventual social isolation is more than sufficient without you adding to their burden. You are trying to help them to fit in, so you need a kind and empathetic approach. Do praise your child every time you see them making the right choice so that you bolster their self-esteem.

The first step is to notice your child when he is in a social group and get him to join-in a group appropriately by "matching his behaviour" to that of the others around them. Explain this to him in detail. For example, if you go into the classroom and everyone is sitting at their desks, do not buzz in like a fly, humming, running, interfering, interrupting and generally being loud; match your behaviour to that of others in your surroundings, sit down at your desk as quietly as you can. If children are shouting, running, jumping and climbing the walls, then it is probably realistic that your child should join-in and not look any different. Look at a variety of different situations with your child and point out what others are doing and explain that if/when they can do this (match their behaviour) too they will enable themselves to fit-in. This can be achieved however it will only come with a bit of maturity and a lot of practice—expect them to not get it right often in the beginning but praise them every time they do. When they don't achieve this; point it out gently and suggest how they might be able to do this in a different way next time. Take them to different environments where different behaviours will be expected, talk about what you might or might not expect when you are there and see if they can achieve it, praise them when they do. I think the phrase, "match your behaviour," might be the single most used phrase in my house! Practice before hand using role play—engage the siblings or cousins, if you have them, reward your child with praise when they get it right. Look at picture books together and see if there are children who are not matching their behaviour in them, see if your child can spot them. Look at the other characters faces and see if anyone has the look of a weird thought.

When we don't match our behaviour, this can lead to weird thoughts and this can have a serious impact on a child's social inclusion.

Weird thoughts: This is a tricky message to deliver without decimating a child's self-esteem, however it will be essential in the long run, because if you don't, others will!! Try and deliver the message as if you were talking about someone else in the first instance, before making your child aware of their own behaviours.

What are weird thoughts and why are they so bad? A weird thought is a preconception; we all have them, about someone based, usually, on the behaviours we observe. For example, licking a window, while this might be perfectly acceptable for a baby, an older child or even adult doing this would give the onlooker a weird thought about that person. It is highly unlikely once you have a weird thought or two, that this individual is going to be top of the guest list for a tea party or sleep over; it may even be that you might try an avoid them all together. Weird thoughts can also be elicited from more common habits such as nose picking, having a good route around the bogies or genitals, especially if hands are not washed. It might not make a person first choice when it comes to picking a partner in games lessons where hands have to be held. Other behaviours that might elicit weird thoughts come from not adhering to the accepted societal norms for example, interrupting, changing the rules of games, pushing in a line, arguing, sulking, not listening to others' points of view, talking incessantly and demonstrating immature behaviour. These are skills that ADHD people struggle with and will have to be worked on so that they can be improved.

The trouble with a weird thought is that once a person has given cause to have them, it can be very difficult for them to be eradicated and a change of mindset to be established, and this message travels like wildfire round a group of peers. Causing isolation and ostracisation, I still hear about children who did strange things in preschool from ten-year-olds and this being cited as the reason for their social ostracisation, *i.e.*, the weird thought still persists and overrides despite all the developmental changes that have occurred since. Where possible match your behaviour so that the all-important weird thoughts are not established or minimised. Your individual ADHD child will have their own individual social problems, make sure you model the desired behaviour, such as winning or losing well, and give them plenty of opportunity to practice getting it right. It will take time for them to adapt, be patient and expect them not to get it right often at first, praise them when you see them trying and encourage them to keep going.

It is very likely that your impulsive ADHD child will be vulnerable to suggestion and manipulation to do silly, reckless or dangerous things. The ADHD child will carry out these things often in the hopes that they can garner social status, prowess and acceptance or friendship from their peer group but, without thinking about the consequences (impulsivity). After the event, they will inevitably get caught, or have been tricked into doing something that makes them look foolish they will be extremely remorseful, but are likely to repeat the behaviour again and not consider the long-term ramifications of their actions, always hoping to be included and not understanding why they are not, although medication can help remediate this. The ADHD child will of course know what the right and wrong thing to do is but the desire, for example, to be accepted may take priority in the heat of the moment; and it is heart-breaking to watch

Often children, especially in a group, can be cruel and will take great pleasure in getting the least popular child to carry out, "tasks" or even bully other children on their behalf, with the promise of great friendship on its conclusion. An immature, vulnerable, socially isolated ADHD child with poor impulse control and a desperation to fit in and become part of a social group is perfect cannon fodder for these types of children. Naturally, the friendship they promise will evaporate and a new and possibly increasing hurdle to their social inclusion will be offered and the ADHD child will take the bait every time. There is no use telling your child that they are not their friends, your child is likely too immature to recognise this and their desperation to fit in will prevent acceptance too. A strategy that might stand in longer term stead is to ask them to get the "friends" to perform the activity first, if they refuse then this is a sure sign that this is not a good idea for your child to follow, so do not perform the task.

Playtimes, lunchtime and downtimes are often the loneliest times for ADHD children, where their rejection by the peer group is emphasised and there is little adult supervision.

## Secret Signs

Chastising a child publicly, in front of family, friends, peer group and other mothers at the school gates can have unfortunate consequences and only goes to prove the point that your child is, in their opinion, naughty, wilful, disobedient and not someone to associate with. It almost certainly will initiate weird thoughts or confirm them for the onlookers.

ADHD children are typically visual learners and we have found the use of two secret signs, one for stop and the other for think, to be very effective. Often ADHD children will not be listening, so you will first have to get their attention by mentioning their name. Once a child knows what the signs are, you will find they are remarkably effective in buying them thinking time, and getting them to alter their behaviour while saving your voice and preserving your child's dignity in public. I have used this discipline technique in sports halls, assemblies and children's parties all without opening my mouth. We use two signs. The first is for STOP, where I hold my index finger up as if I'm going to ask a question. This means STOP everything you're doing, look around you. The second looks like I'm making the sign for OK. This means THINK, think if what you're doing is OK, matching your behaviour. These have worked so well for us and it is not any kind of public remediation of his behaviour. So well, in fact, that his then year three teacher used our sign for stop, wanting to get the classes attention, and couldn't understand why he was the only member of his class who actually stopped.

## Running Off

As any mother of a toddler knows, running off is a parent's worst nightmare! It is inappropriate to have an older child on reigns, although I have threatened this on more than one occasion. ADHD children quite likely to unthinkingly do this, attracted by the moment! Far better to make it into a game, where you are in control. ADHD children like to wander off and feel the freedom of not being tethered physically or metaphorically to their parents, just as their peers do. It is also an outward display of parental trust. Let them know that you are confident that they will return when you say and tell them if they don't there will be the consequence of them not being allowed to go free again. They will want to live up to the responsibility and the challenge. This is for their own safety.

A very real danger for the ADHD child is strangers and enticement. They will need much greater supervision than the average child, especially in public places, swimming pools, beaches and parks as they are more vulnerable to suggestion. It is very important to discuss with the child to see what their perception of a stranger is. I was horrified when I checked with my own child to discover that he thought a stranger was only ever a man and that even then once he knew the man's name, he would no longer be a stranger, he was 8 at the time. Be very careful to ensure that your child knows what danger looks like and give them tips (the NSPCC is a great resource) to keep themselves safe. Even with all the knowledge check in on the child to make sure that they really understand. An ADHD child is more likely to succumb to the suggestion of sweets or a puppy if they follow a stranger.

Tell your child they may go as far as… insert something here that the child will have to look for or count, such as three cars on the corner or the green fence, or the large tree. When you say, "Boomerang" the child is to return to you as fast as possible, so they must practise listening. This works really well for the child; it is a measured independence and they will enjoy returning to you when you cry, "Boomerang", this should be heavily praised when achieved. Remember they will also be doing lots of running so it will hopefully have tired them out and you might even get some rest as a result later on! This works best from about the age of six and can be a fond game that you can play for many years to come.

## Playdates, Parties and Social Gatherings.

*What happens if your child is never invited or children don't want to come to your house? How to help and what to do?*

For that all-important social life to occur we must be social! No one will want to invite a child who hurts others, breaks objects (even by mistake) or doesn't value others property. Make sure the discipline techniques are well underway before you commence.

When we have other people's children in our homes, we expect on their departure to have some untidiness but the house and furniture and belongings should remain intact. It is acceptable that toys will occasionally get broken, but wilful and wanton destruction is wholly inappropriate behaviour and will result in the end of invitations rapidly. As will hurting other children, even if the intent was friendly.

Have high expectations of your child's behaviour. At home do not let them bounce on beds and sofas, these are expensive items which people do not replace frequently in their homes. Windows do not need to be slid down, nor do they require touching—unless you want to clean them every day. Electronics, such as washing machines should not be tampered with. Phones are private and not to be fiddled with. Respecting people's bedrooms, bathrooms and personal spaces is also a must. Cupboards and drawers should not be opened and rifled through. Food must be offered by the host and not snatched and grabbed at. Other families will not thank you if these bad manners occur—and they may have weird thoughts. Remember you are a guest-behave like one! Manners maketh the man!!! These are hard rules which should be followed no matter how familiar the host is or how much they insist that it doesn't matter. Sadly, the ADHD child has to have higher expectations than the rest of society often because there is a predisposition towards always assuming the negative about them.

Have your child model the expected behaviours at home, frequently, so they have a chance to become automatic. If you are lucky enough to be invited to a party or tea, stay with your child to facilitate the fledgling social life, this doesn't mean be your child's shadow, just means being the room "helping" the hostess and keeping a distant eye. Arrange this with hostess in advance. Offer to bring the pudding. Always help tidy up and insist your child helps too. Make sure your child uses his manners and thanks to hostess on departure. Manners go a long way to improving others' perception of you. A disruptive child that has manners is far easier to accept and warm to. It is akin to the examiner that is marking 100 papers; if yours is paper number 99 after a long hot day of marking in June, and you have scrawled your way across the page, with many scrubbings out, even if the content is there, the examiner is only human and may not be as favourable. So, it is important to remember that your host may be busy, tired and stressed out, we all have lives, make sure you are not allowing your child to, "scrawl" through the host's home or their child's birthday party. If they do ensure your child apologises and remediates their behaviour or you leave quickly—don't be surprised if you are not invited again for a while.

Most important, keep it short, leave all concerned wanting more. There is nothing worse than a guest out-staying their welcome, and you will more likely have a return visit if you leave on a high. Reciprocate, but have a plan. Have lots of agreed in advance activities to keep everyone busy. Make sure your child is well-aware of what is and is not permitted. Do not allow children upstairs or in rooms with doors shut. Only allow one child to go to the toilet at one time. Sounds obvious, but the ADHD child may have a lack of idea of personal space, or the children could be silly in the smallest room of the house. Your guests might not have realised about your child's ADHD or you might not want them to know. If this is the case make sure any references to it, such as notes on calendars or appointment letters on fridges are removed and put in a safe place. Have lots of snacks available even if you are not inviting the child for dinner. Make sure you have a reason for terminating the play date, especially if the other party are unaware of your child's ADHD, otherwise they might think it is a bit odd that you are asking them to leave when the children are having so much fun.

Carefully plan when these rendezvous are to occur and the motives behind the other family's offer of friendship or playdate. It could be that they are coming to see how awful this child really is—it has happened to me. If your child becomes very tired and or overstimulated at school, it is highly likely that they will not cope well with a playdate after school and it might be an unmitigated disaster. Remember you are in control of who comes into your home, which is also your child's personal space. Unless you are very sure about the other person, you do not have to invite them into your inner sanctum. It might be useful alternative to meet at a park or playground or some other space where your child and their, "friend" can have shared experiences which will help foster long-term friendship, and where you can get to know the other parent without leaving yourself feeling vulnerable. I will discuss the other parents at school later.

## Take home messages

- Agree with your child what behaviours need to be changed and what the consequences will be.
- Be consistent, follow your own rules!
- Be fair, do not move the goal posts by increasing the punishment, do include all other children in the household. Praise if all has gone well.
- Don't escalate situations, be matter of fact and non-judgemental.
- Be realistic before you start, remember this is a marathon and not a sprint, Rome was not built in a day.
- Have high expectations of behaviour.
- Be positive, your child can crack this!
- Be compassionate, you are not their jailer you are their parent, tell them how much you love them and how proud you are of them often, these might be the only kind words that they have heard all day.

You and your child are in this together.

# SIBLINGS

The relationships between siblings are notoriously difficult, perhaps even more so with a neurodivergent child in the family. It is important for all children to feel loved, valued and safe, this way they can thrive. The ADHD child is significantly more immature, typically three to five years emotionally less mature than their chronological age and will be more demanding of a caregiver's time. It is therefore easy to see how friction can occur. It is essential that the home promotes tolerance and is fair to all the children. Encourage all family members to celebrate even the smallest success, and good social skills; something that ADHD children often lack often lack. If there are, for example, exercises or homework to be done include all the children so that it becomes a team event, encourage them to praise each other. It is very likely that there will be other experts involved with your child and not just a paediatrician, these could be SALT (speech and language therapy), OT (occupational therapy and CBT (cognitive behavioural therapy, as a child grows older), each of these specialists will give your child exercises to do at home to practice.

Try and create space and time within the home for each child, especially if they share a bedroom. Do not compare your children, the ADHD child will already be berating themselves on their failings and will be well- aware of their shortcomings. Saying things like, "Why can't you do this? Your little brother can." is not helpful or productive. Also, asking questions as a competition amongst siblings may be seen as a harmless and fun activity to a parent, but where one child has ADHD, especially if it is the older one, it is very undermining if younger/ non-ADHD child can publicly demonstrate he is more able to answer them. These instances are counterproductive and will only serve to form divisions within the family. Remember your ADHD child will have been compared all day at school and will need a positive space to retreat into. Pointing out their obvious failings will only bring distance between you. Treat each child on their own merits, every child has some redeeming features; mention them often and publicly, this will promote cohesion between children and increase the already fragile self-esteem of the ADHD child.

Inevitably your children will need discipline, be sure to be fair, and make the punishment, if needed, fits the crime.

## You can't cut yourself in two

You are one human being, not several, do not beat yourself up over things you cannot achieve. At some points during their childhood each of your children will deservedly require more of your attention than at others. Be honest with your children and explain this to them in as simple a way as possible. For example, we have a child who has exams to sit, his brothers know that I have to devote my time to helping him at least once per day. If your older child has homework to do, which requires your attention, have the little ones sit at the table and do quiet activities, such as drawing, colouring, or writing puzzles next to you. This way you are able to give your attention to the child having to work and occupy the other children.

## Division of duties

Have children in the household perform light tasks, this will make your life easier for you and it will give them responsibility, after all we are training our children to eventually be self-sufficient. Make sure these are duties to be carried out on a regular basis, but are achievable. Ensure there will be a no-blame consequence if they are not performed, e.g., if the dishwasher is not unpacked and there are no clean knives to use, sit there with plates of food and say, "Well, how are we going to eat dinner?" This will work even better if children have to jointly perform tasks, that way you will be developing team work and social skills.

## He ain't heavy he's my brother—explaining differences to other children

Have the attitude that you are more than just a family, you are in fact a team. There are plenty of books available to explain ADHD to children, that are easy to understand, e.g., "All dogs have ADHD" by Kathy Hoopman; it is a fun picture-based book that simply explains what ADHD is to small children. Be mindful to only give a child information that they are emotionally equipped to cope with. Do not suggest their sibling is somehow less or dysfunctional, but do pick some of their behaviours and explain that they cannot help them.

Promote the idea that it is the family's role to help them overcome the difficulties together. Answer any questions they might have truthfully and explain that you understand that sometimes their sibling can be high-maintenance. Reiterate how much you love your children and how proud you are of them, moreover how much joy it brings to you when you see them helping each other to be the best that they can be.

## Games to increase social skills at home

Social skills are often rather lacking in ADHD people. They tend to talk non-stop, appearing selfish or self-obsessed, they fiddle with objects more out of curiosity than malice, they don't like to lose, they think they know best, the list goes on. Here are some tips:

**Food**: Buy a small cake (enough for two), have one child cut the cake in half, allow the other child to pick their piece of cake first. This will promote fair division of the treat, if the child doesn't cut the cake fairly then it is to be expected that they will get less of the treat. Have a matter-of-fact tone if this turns out to be the case. Promote the idea that thigs should be fair by explaining it to them explicitly.

Have your children make a cake or bread together, under your supervision. Make sure they take turns at each stage.

**Learning based games**:

- If there are words to learn to read, spellings and times tables to practise etc (there always are) try and teach your children, if possible, together. For example, at the end of year 1 there is The National Phonics Test. In this test children will have to learn how to read and spell words, some of them will be nonsense words, using the phonics they have learnt. Each year group also has its own Phonemes, spelling rules and exception words to learn. Give your children a set of cards (these can be purchased) with the beginnings and endings of words, e.g., Fl and ight. Make sure you give the ADHD child the set that they struggle with the most, (but with a few that they can do). Have them each turn over a card and ask them together to sound it out, ask them to decide together if this is a real or nonsense word and then tell you. Sit with them while they are doing this. This approach also works for number bonds, times tables and general spellings. Praise your children for showing teamwork and losing or winning appropriately. Mention their strengths and weaknesses explicitly, evolve the game so that it doesn't become mundane and they feel the success. This will only work if they are similar age and/or ability. If they are not there is a grave danger of making oldest feel like a public failure if the younger sibling can do as well or better. In this scenario it is better to play against an adult who gets words "wrong" at times!! Try to get your child to beat their own score. Always have some already known words in the piles. Lots of repetition, of the items to be learnt but also the social skill that is being practiced.

- Another game for simple addition and social skills is Pontoon, allow each child to be the banker in turn, model explicitly the behaviour when you win or lose.
- Matching pairs, have your children team up against you, so that they work cooperatively, this can be adapted for phonics and number learning.

**Communication, Listening and Language Skills**: Have a pile of Lego (Duplo might be more suitable) divide the pile so each child has the same colour and shaped bricks. Have your children sit back-to-back, ask child one to build a simple model using no more than 5 bricks. Then ask them to describe their model and have the other child build it based on their descriptions. See who gets closest. This encourages stepwise instruction following, listening skills and develops language skills. The same can be done with a simple drawing on paper. This also helps language, directional language and vocabulary

**Reading**: Have your children, (if they are able), read with you a story, each taking a page, paragraph or chapter. You could each listen and help to read their own books in turn. Also ask about what has happened before in the story before you begin to check that they have remembered. Ask explicitly about what they predict might come next and any inference in the story. Undoubtedly, your ADHD child will struggle with this task. Point out explicitly where they might find the inference. Encourage your child to sit as still as they can during this time, use a weighted blanket, which can help the ADHD child feel calm and keep them still. if necessary, praise them for joining in. Be mindful to keep the time short and make sure that you do most of the reading, this will ensure you maintain their attention and they find it an enjoyable experience. If your child doesn't want to play because they are not feeling in the mood or because they are afraid of public failure don't make an issue, just perform the task with other child play and appear to be having fun, they will often decide they want to join-in

## Reward and discipline for siblings.

Rewards and discipline for ADHD children and their siblings may seem harsh, but it's tough love. ADHD children need firm boundaries and a greater amount of explanation so that they can match their behaviour and fit in. The real world is an unfair and harsh place for non -conformers. So, they either learn to conform to the majority or they will be found by the bullies, manipulators and will be excluded by the peer group. Especially for a younger sibling their role model will be your ADHD child, this might mean that they will also need a larger amount of discipline as they will copy the behaviour of their sibling.

At some point during any child's life, you will need to impose, "discipline", this is not the same as punishment (as explained earlier) but to teach. Discipline needs to be imposed before self-discipline can occur. Self-discipline is one of the most important and useful skills that everyone needs to possess. It is a skill is essential in every area of life. Using common sense, thinking before acting and prioritising are harder for ADHD children who don't always connect cause and effect; and in turn their siblings who mimic them. It is vital for achieving goals and carrying out tasks to the end. This means perseverance and not giving up when things get tough. Making wise and healthy choices. Implement discipline in small steps with achievable goals. Make sure that you are fair. Just because your ADHD child is emotionally less mature does not mean that they can get away with bad behaviour; you should have high expectations from your children at all times. It also means no child in the family should be perceived as getting easier treatment. Discipline will work best to promote cohesion between siblings if it is used globally.

"Manners maketh the man", encourage your child to use them! An awful lot of good will can be achieved with the outside world if a, "please" and a, "thank you" are attached! It also serves to show the rest of the world that you and your child/children are trying your hardest to conform. People will look more favourably on a child with manners, and this is something that the ADHD child needs in copious amounts. Even when this is something your ADHD child struggles with, if the other members of the household have and use their manners, it will go a long way to alter people's perception of you all.

Rewarding good behaviour in children, does not have to mean sweets or toys, in fact I am not a huge fan of rewards being tangible. Kind words are sometimes much more effective, and they are free!

For your non-ADHD child, concurrently impose any discipline technique being used on your ADHD child, and have the same consequences. If rules are broken have a matter-of-fact tone, state the rule and the consequence with as little emotion as possible. This will hopefully lead to less confrontation and it will be an outward display of equality amongst your children. Be sure to point out to your children when rules have been flouted, and that the consequence is being imposed. This way they will all know you are prepared to follow through and you will affect a speedier behaviour change. Praise your non-ADHD child in equal amounts also when things go well.

## It's not fair

No, it's not fair. It's not fair you are older, it's not fair you are younger, it's not fair they have ADHD. Life is not fair; we are not born equal. Remind your child of all the things they can do with ease and the great efforts their sibling ADHD has to put in to achieve the same result; remind them that this is the truer description of not being fair. Tell them how proud you are of them, and how lucky their sibling is to have you. Promote tolerance and cohesion as much as possible.

## When siblings have a party or a playdate

This is tough! It is very often that your non-ADHD child will be included in parties and playdates when your ADHD child will not. It really is very difficult for the child left out and can cause friction and resentment along-with exacerbating feelings of loneliness and isolation. I cannot count the number of times I have had a heartbroken child at home ruminating on the fact that he hasn't been to a single birthday party all year and yet his brother is on his tenth one this term. A sad but, often-all-too true fact of life for an ADHD child.

Ask your other child not to brag or draw attention to this; quietly explain that their sibling is feeling sad about the lack of a social life. There is nothing worse nor more likely to cause an argument of cataclysmic proportions than jealousy. Encourage your other child to share, the party bag and cake. If you have playdates at home, make sure you ask the mother to attend too, unless you really know the child well. During this time increase your ADHD child's, "street-cred", by offering them a tablet to play on. This they will be fixated on this and will play quietly with and not disturb the activities of the other children. This will allow the other parents to see your child at their calmest and quietest.

Make sure you offer plenty of food that the other child will like, enquire what this is beforehand. Ensure that you tell your ADHD child that he needs to let his sibling play with his friend. Do not allow two children to gang up on another, or the ADHD child to take-over and change the rules or dictate the rules of a game. This will lead to conflict. Have pre-agreed consequences if this does happen; make sure you follow through. Do not allow your child to be bullied or be a bystander in their own home. Do not allow the children upstairs where this could happen unnoticed. This is very hard if ADHD child is younger as they will naturally want to join in with bigger children.

## School for Siblings

Have an open dialogue, where possible, about the challenges your non-neurodivergent child faces at home. It may well be that you have a highly empathetic child who is very tolerant of idiosyncrasy. It is highly likely that a sibling will feel protective, especially when they are younger, but will lose patience with their sibling as they get older. Ensure you and school do not abuse this by giving them too much responsibility towards their sibling at school. Additionally, these children have enough at home without being sat next to an ADHD child at school. However, you may have an angry child who shows mirror behaviour of its sibling, this can happen with a younger sibling is copying unfortunate role model, if this is the case make sure global techniques are employed so that the child is well aware of the boundaries and consequences.

# SCHOOL

At some point your ADHD child will enter into the institution of school. This can be a daunting prospect for you both. You may have had previous unhappy experiences in these institutions. You may feel you know the local schools well, or maybe new to the area and have no knowledge. Schools change over the years. Teachers and leadership change along with the curriculum, so whatever preconceived ideas you might or might not have investigate the options available to you thoroughly.

School days, contrary to the phrase, are often not the happiest days of our lives. This is particularly true of primary school where children are forced into relatively close environments, studying all aspects of the curriculum with a cohort not of their choosing or similar academic ability, but by a simple accident of their birth and geographical location.

Reasons for choosing a school might be based on location, siblings, money available or even how much wrap-around care they can provide. Young children are typically not interested in world events, they are interested in their world, which is micro rather than macro and often solely revolves around school. While school days might not always be the happiest, they are some of the most important in helping a child learn how to interact with their peer group and get along in the world. For your child school is their world, it is vital that this environment is nurturing and understanding.

## The individual child

Although you will have undoubtedly realised this, it is important to remember that your child is an individual and so are their needs. What might suit one of your children will not necessarily suit them all. Furthermore, you may have more than one child with additional or special needs remember too that these children are individuals and they will have their own unique strengths and weaknesses. There is no one size fits all approach.

## What to look for in a school

The best schools are open and honest about their premises. They will welcome you in and listen to any concerns without being judgemental or claiming that they have many times met and taught children just like yours. They might well have had ADHD students in the past, but it is as ludicrous to say that they have had girls attend their school (unless it is an all-boys school), your child is an individual, they will have never taught your child before.

A good school will allow you, if you ask, to speak with other special needs parents to see how they feel about the school, how they manage to meet their child's needs and how they provide a safe learning environment. Be careful that this is truly transparent arrangement. I have the experience of meeting a family whose child had and ADHD diagnosis, only to find that his symptoms were not severe and that the parent was a governor at the school. I should have run for the hills then, but I didn't I wanted to believe this was going to be a panacea. My son lasted nearly two terms.

Any school that has 100 pupils and claims not to have any children with ADHD is either lying or has no clue about what the signs and symptoms are. Remember ADHD affects approximately 1 in 5 children and adults or 20 %, to varying degrees. In all likelihood there will be at least one other child attending your child's school or prospective that has ADHD.

If your child has a diagnosis a good school will not have the, "Let him start and we will wait and see what support he needs approach." Rather they will already have an action plan where they will give your child almost too much support and then slowly withdraw it to see how they can facilitate them managing independently. Be very cautious about proceeding with enrolment if the former is the case, it could be set up for failure.

A school that provides structure during the day and in the forms of games or clubs at unstructured times, such as break time, for all pupils is key. Have a very careful look around their playground —this is where social problems are likely to occur. Ask the school to provide you with information about playtime and lunchtime arrangements.

The school may or may not have any understanding of your child's condition, but that should not be a prerequisite, although it does help. You should feel that staff members, not just the SENCO have a willingness to listen and an open mind about educating themselves. It may be that you will have to help them substantially in this endeavour, provided they are open about their shortcomings, but provide you with assurance that they to want to learn it should not form a barrier to your child attending.

Teachers in the UK often have very little training about special needs. Whichever school your child attends you will need to educate them about your individual child. Your child is not a pamphlet nor are they a check list of symptoms and school should recognise that a mother knows their child best.

A good school will be understanding about medication and be willing to allow the child to be supported to take any medicines required during the school day. They will be able to store it in a safe place. They should show discretion when the child takes the medication. When filling in forms and questionnaires for paediatricians they should show, not only the utmost care and attention to the questions asked, but make sure that any information remains private. I will never know which family was the recipient of my sons ADHD questionnaire, filled in by his then Year Two teacher; to say I was angry was an understatement.

The SENCO should want to have a separate meeting with you,

away from the class teacher and Head. This will allow for an open discussion before you decide to sign up. Beware of any school that shrouds the SENCO in mystery, you need to know that this individual is someone who you can work with and have a happy relationship with. The SENCO should be kind but firm and have a clear idea about what support they are able to put in place for your child. They should also know about external agencies and services available in the local area that can offer additional support too.

School, and class teachers in particular, should understand there is more impact on an ADHD child's life than merely the academic element. In fact, if the social element is addressed, the child will feel nurtured and supported by their cohort and barriers to learning might not occur. Good support for social skills should be in evidence throughout their day-to-day activities. Additionally, school will understand the lag between your child's chronological age and their social ability, remember it is 3-5 years, so a ten-year-old will be more like a 5 or 7-year-old in their behaviour.

School should have a clear Behaviour Management Policy and SEND Policy, which should be freely available for parents and carers to see. High standards of expected behaviour should be set and maintained. They should have clear outlines of consequences meted out for poor behaviour and they should be consistent. This should not be draconian or punitive in nature. Ask the school what they can offer to help your child. Interview them. Do not just visit the potential school in a new parents' group, ask for a separate meeting with the Head and SENCO. If this isn't forthcoming and the SENCO is too "busy" …walk away. A child thrives best when parents and teachers are in harmony, if you get the feeling that this might not be possible walk away and find another school. It is, often, very distressing for child when there is acrimony between home and school. When talking to a prospective school expect them to say that you will need to take an active role and be involved in all strategies applied to your child and see SEND agreements, from the outset.

The suggestion of attending part-time is a great in the beginning, for a week or so, so that the child will reduce their anxiety and learn the routines of the school.

## Mainstream Private Schools

If you are in the fortunate position to be able to afford a mainstream private school you may think that this is a better or more superior choice for your child. You may be thinking that smaller class sizes and individual attention, along with all the extra-curricular activities on offer, will provide the perfect opportunity for your child to thrive.

It could be that you have a very bright child, as evidenced by an Educational Psychologist, and your child will pass entrance tests with ease. These schools will certainly become very enthusiastic about a high IQ in a potential customer. If you have an older child this statement is true, however, when a child is preschool or EYFS they are too young for a diagnosis. Private schools will usually accept all children at the EYFS stage, but your child may be asked to leave once a diagnosis has been given.

Be *very* cautious. Private schools can contain teachers who have not received any extra training to join their individual institutions. The grounds might look pretty, the swimming pool massive and the uniform impressive. However, these can conceal a multitude of minefields for the ADHD child. Beautiful old buildings and vast expanses of gardens take money to maintain. Large quantities of full-time peripatetic teachers require full-time salaries; their overheads are huge. These schools are, in essence, businesses; they trade on their reputations at being able to get children into the right public schools or tertiary educational establishments. While I am not saying they do not care, they cater mainly to the middle-bright sector of society, with no disabilities. They, typically, are not best suited to any kind of exotic special need, such as ADHD or ASD; but they might be ok for dyslexia—unless they specifically mention them on their prospectus or website—there are some that do.

They might claim to have experience, they might even get excellent results from your child; this could eventually come at the cost of the happiness of your child—you can't square a circle. They are results driven and if the top grades are not achieved this will have a significant impact on the potential foot fall through reception, in the shape of fresh new parents willing to sign on the dotted line, and therefore the businesses' bank balance. Although you may have to pay the equivalent of the national debt to them any additional support will come at an extra cost. They may not even be able to offer any extra support, or not suitable to support your child.

I have recently heard of a school promising a child a place, and allowing the parents to differ entry to reception class for a year, well beyond the cut-off date for applications to primary school admission. The child received a formal diagnosis of ADHD and the place was instantly withdrawn. The parents were left to look for another school, for their now special needs child, from the places that had yet to be filled by the local authority. This school had in total met this child no less than three times before allowing the parents to secure a place *via* non-refundable deposit in the Reception Class and before diagnosis. In the prospectus, this school claims to value the individual needs of the child, the ISI (independent schools inspectorate) have rated them as Outstanding. I can assure you that this is a far from outstanding institution with the interest of the individual child at their hearts. I could go on, but I hope you have gathered a flavour of my opinion.

I am not trying to suggest that all private schools are bad. However, you will need to look very carefully and decide if it truly is the right option for your child. There are several specialist private schools which pride themselves on being able to cater for children with ADHD and proudly mention this on their websites. These schools, if you have the resources, would definitely be interesting options. I would advise you to research heavily and think carefully.

If you decide on this option ask about the experience and qualifications of staff, especially the SENCO. Enquire about the number of ADHD children they have and where they have gone on to after they have left. A good school will ask to see reports from the current school and conduct their own observations. They might insist on having the child in school for a trial period, which from your side is a risky approach. If you decide to go ahead ask for the names of other parents with ADHD children there, but be sure this is a truly transparent arrangement.

## What support is available

The amount of support your child will require is individual to your child, and dependant on recommendations by the specialist team you have working with you. State schools need to provide the first five thousand pounds worth of support from a notional amount of their budget and have to have strong evidence in order to apply for high needs funding (HNF). This does not mean to say that they have to foot the bill for this support. If you are able to pay or contribute then the school can use this as evidence to apply for high needs funding. If you plan on applying for an EHCP (Educational Health Care Plan) this will be vital in your application. EHPC's can be initiated by parents, school or a combination. There are specialists available in all areas of the country that can help you fill in the forms and help you advocate for your child.

## Teamwork

The best results for the child are when school and parents work together as a team. The child will feel nurtured, supported and secure, they will also know that there is a global approach to their difficulties leaving little grey area and room for manoeuvre. You and your child's teachers should aim for honest and open dialogues with each other, and you should be able to approach them about any subject.

In July, before the academic year ends and reports and children come flying out of the school gates, I make two appointments. The first I make with the teacher for the following academic year, the second I make with the SENCO, in that order.

I like a friendly chat with the prospective teacher. This is my opportunity to gauge them and introduce myself in a state of calm; where I am composed and where I can tell them a little bit about my child and how he functions best. I will pass on information about my child's ADHD and ADHD classroom management (there are books available), along with any relevant specialist's letters.

Usually, she will have received notes about him, obviously they will know him from being in school and will have spoken to their colleagues so they will have already formed an initial opinion. I go to great lengths to thank them for their time before we begin and tell them that I don't want to be in their classroom in the next academic year any more than they probably want me there, and that with the right approach they will seldom see me. I listen to them very carefully when I ask the salient questions, which are:

1. Have you any experience with special needs, particularly ADHD?
2. These are the accommodations or adjustments that have previously worked in other classrooms.
3. What accommodations have you made for children like mine in the past and what worked best in your experience?
4. What will be the changes in expectation that my child can anticipate, such as homework every night?

I might also mention any specific issues with the peer group at this stage so she, and it's often a "she", is aware of them, for example if my child has been bullied, or doesn't work well with an individual.

I mention my child's specific strengths and weakness and I labour the point that I will work with him and school to assist them in any way possible. I make it *very clear* that this needs to happen and that she and I need to keep each-other informed. I do not expect to attend parents' evening to be met with a barrage of

ADHD symptoms that she needs to have made me aware of at the earliest possible opportunity; or that my child has been failing in a particular subject for months at school without my prior knowledge. Parents' evening should not be Newsnight, there should be no nasty surprises! Nicely, pleasantly, I leave the teacher knowing that I do not want to live in her classroom, that I have confidence in her ability, but that I will be seeing her much more frequently than we would both like if I feel the measures put-in-place are not working. I try go in positively at the initial class teacher meeting. A pleasant and appreciative approach that will hopefully set the tone for the year ahead.

I then have my meeting with the SENCO, she and I will have a close relationship and will have met many times before. I will always make sure that she is included in Christmas and end of year gifts. I make sure that we have the best possible working relationship. Depending on the outcomes of my meeting with the new teacher I will mention any potential red flags I can foresee in their (my child and new teachers) future relationship and ask the SENCO if she can monitor the situation if necessary. The SENCO will already know that I will be a thorn in everyone's side if I feel my child's needs are not being met, usually because it deprives me of significant amounts of sleep!

## What does a good teacher look like?

A good teacher, like a good school, will listen to your concerns with genuine compassion. She will want to know before you have to tell her, what subjects and activities your child likes best. She will already know that you want your child to conform, let her know you will do whatever you can to assist her and allow your child to thrive. It will make her job much easier too if you can work together as a team.

She will ask you what disciplinary measures you implement at home and will want to have a global approach. She might share with you the methods or phraseology she uses so that you can implement them at home too.

She will outline any significant changes your child can expect to experience in her classroom, such as homework.

She will understand the importance of having positive social relationships and will be keen to facilitate or preserve them for your child. She might already know if there have been difficulties and will want to reassure you that she will try and accommodate your child where possible.

She will tell you that she has an open-door policy and that you are welcome at any point. Do not abuse this! Only see her when it is absolutely necessary.

She will suggest that you sit down together at the end of the second week after the start of school in September; and will want to know how you feel your child is progressing and you are both coping.

She will know lots of details about your child and will have read the previous teacher's notes and relevant literature. You will feel very confident, that even if she knows very little about SEND, she will go to great lengths to support you and your child.

As a result, you will rarely feel the need to see her, apart from parents evening. Your child will flourish and you will be sad that she is no longer your child's teacher in July.

## What makes an inadequate Teacher

If only prospective teachers were given a psychometric test to see if it is a job that would be suitable for them and the mental health of the general population. Teachers are in charge of one of the population's most vulnerable groups, namely children, perhaps doubly so if you factor in a SEND child. They can wield an almighty power and have the ability to set the tone of relationships both within and outside of the classroom. Not all teachers are born equal, regardless of their educational setting, some do not have compassion or empathy, or not enough. Truer however is that many do not have adequate training in SEND, however this alone does not make them inadequate teachers.

The inadequate teacher will have met your SEND child before, and will have a fixed mindset on how they are to be dealt with. They will not need to read the literature because they already know everything. They don't recognise or understand what they are looking at and attribute it to poor parenting or just a naughty child—the myth still prevails.

They may not even believe ADHD actually exists. I will never forget looking through my son's personal school file as he completed Year 1; it was a shamble with tatty post-its and scraps of observations, completed by the former SENCO and his Reception teacher. On one of these bits of paper I found the words "spoiled brat" in her handwriting. The current SENCO, who was looking with me, said what I was thinking "nefarious—I'm so sorry", I was horrified and devastated. This Reception teacher is now a Head a Prep School in the South of England.

They may be overly critical and unfair on your child, punishing and blaming them for perceived poor behaviour publicly. Naturally your child will be labelled as, "naughty" by his classmates, soon to follow suit will be their parents.

They will have low expectations of your child academically and no understanding of the impairment of being socially immature.

They will have tardiness in filling in questionnaires for paediatricians' appointments.

They might even deliberately fill in questionnaires saying that they see no symptoms blocking your child's route to diagnosis.

They will have very little concern about the problems your child faces during unstructured time because they do not recognise this as an essential part of school life.

They will give you the general feeling of a lack of compassion, you are a nuisance and neurotic, and your child lacks discipline and is disruptive. You might actually feel they actively dislike your child. They will see you often. However, you will not be able to change their approach. It will be a difficult year. It would seem in the experience of other ADHD mums I have talked to, and myself, that there may be at least one teacher like this in every school—if you're lucky!

What can you do? Get a tutor, see the SENCO, wait it out—if it is likely that the following year there will be a good teacher. If things are really too unbearable, move school—a year is a long time. Although, as one teacher said to me once, "Your child's problems will follow you wherever you go. My answer to this now, Headmaster was, "Yes, they will, but the right environment makes the problems dissipate significantly because you're not facing them alone." He was a teacher who severely lacked compassion.

## A Note to Parents

Thankfully, the majority of teachers want to see a child in their care thrive academically and form positive, meaningful and lasting friendships with their cohort. It makes their lives easier, rather than battling World War Three daily.

Teachers have a duty of care to all the children in their class, to ensure their pupils are educated and their needs are being met. They often have 30 children of varying abilities and disabilities in their class who have needs they have to meet; your child might not be the only one with SEND in their care. They are time deficient people trying to do a difficult job.

Try, where you can, to make their lives easier. Do not demand more from them than is reasonable. If they are covering a topic in your child's class, ask them if there are any areas of learning and pre learning that you could go over to help your child. Be appreciative of what they have to do, foster the good relationship.

## How to communicate with school—the squeaky wheel gets the grease

When you have to meet with school always send a *quick* and *friendly*, email to summarise the meeting. Make sure you copy yourself in so they know you are keeping records.

If anything was unclear in the meeting, this is the time to ask the questions.

It maybe that you need to email the school without first having a meeting. For example, unkindness in the playground. If this is the case make sure you read any appropriate policies on the school's website and quote them in your email. Begin by pleasantly enquiring and find out what has gone on. You cannot always assume your child's perceptions are exactly correct even if they are convinced that this is what happened.

There is always time to up the anti-later, if necessary. It is far better to resolve matters in a calm, understanding way, unless the situation is very serious.

## A Note to Teachers

The child in you class, that might drive you to distraction, is loved by someone. This is easy for teachers to forget, particularly at the end of a very stressful day.

Most parents love their children very much. This child may be making your job difficult; running amok in your classroom and causing havoc, but you must choose your words carefully, every child has some redeeming features; even if they are very small. Relationships can quickly become impaired and it may be very difficult, if not impossible to repair the damage that a few careless words, at the end of a long day, can cause. I remember my child's teacher telling me on the afternoon of the first day of the academic year that, after he had pushed over the child who had bullied him for nearly a year, she was not sure if further sanctions would be taken. I still haven't forgotten that; school chose not to prevent or notice the bullying and taunting from persisting in the first place and then considered imposing sanctions on the victim!

If you are dealing with a family who has a fresh diagnosis, recognise that the parents will have to go through the process of understanding and eventually acceptance of their child's condition.

Typically, parents will experience grief as they slowly realise that the future, they had anticipated for their child is now gone forever and a long road of problems, and potentially other diagnoses, may lie ahead. They will be bombarded with information, statistics and facts, which might be terrifying. Be compassionate and offer support, remind them about the positive traits their child exhibits. Make them realise that you are part of their team and that you want to help create an environment in which their child can thrive.

Parents may be angry and looking for a reason to explain their child's behaviours. They may demand much of your time, have unrealistic expectations and blame you and the school for all their child's faults. Always make sure you listen to them, accommodate them where possible. Understand that they are frustrated and frightened of the future. There may be no significant improvement in their child, despite all the effort they feel they have put in. Suggest an action plan that you can implement together, a global approach.

Parents may become depressed and feel like they have caused the child's problems. They will feel overwhelmed with the issues they are facing and not know where to start—they are most likely to be exhausted too. Make sure you remember the child's redeeming features and remind the parents of them. Help the parents think of solutions and an action plan. The parents may be too tired and lack understanding or knowledge to be able to think of one themselves and are so overburdened with information they will not know where to start.

Eventually, the parents will realise it is not all doom and gloom, they will start to celebrate the child that they have and not the one they have lost. They will embrace their child's idiosyncrasies and differences as part of their unique make up and take on the world. Be mindful that they will be extremely protective of their child. They will be difficult if you do not reach their expectations of support for their child. If you work with the parents, they will often be your biggest allies and they will fall over themselves to help and assist you in whatever way they can.

## Extra-curricular Activities

Your ADHD child will have had an exhausting day at school, trying to match their behaviour and not give people weird thoughts, as well as trying their best to achieve in the lessons. Conforming like this all day is exhausting for the child.

It may well be that they do not have positive peer relationships. Although they might like the idea of clubs and activities after school ask yourself is more of the same beneficial or might it be detrimental to them. If it is a team sport, such as football, how will your tired and overstimulated child feel if they are the last one picked for the team again. Will their peer group blame them if the goals are not scored? How would this make your child feel? It is likely that this will have a damaging effect on their self-esteem. They have to attend school with their cohort, they do not have to spend their free time with them.

Find clubs and activities that are not part of school. Perhaps where being a team player is not a perquisite, cycling club, athletics, karate are all good choices. I would avoid Scouts and Brownies; these are run by lovely and well-meaning but often uneducated in the world of SEND mums. It could do more harm than good if it goes wrong.

## Other Mothers and their Children

It is easy to forget, until we get there, that when our children start school we too are starting. Inevitably, you will meet the other parents while dropping your child off or collecting them from school. Often you will have no more in common with each other than the fact that you are mothers. I wish I could tell you that they will recognise that you are trying your hardest and obviously love your child. I also wish I could say that they are willing to tolerate all children, differences and all. However, this is often the most stressful part of my day.

The social ostracisation and exclusion your child faces daily will meet you as you wait with your child in the mornings before school and to be released at the end of the day, and believe me you will feel it, it can be very real.

You will see the "look" some mothers give you as your child 'kicks off" That look implies, "Don't go near you might catch it". I have seen it many times children are quickly spirited away from you and your child; leaving you to think that you are wearing some kind of repellent, that only they know exists. You and your child have been labelled; it is quite possible that this emanates from the classroom. if you have teacher who is less than adequate on your hands. Even if you don't your child will find their own mischief and naturally will be called out more than the average child. Children of a certain ages will pick-up on any unusual behaviour patterns and love to be little policemen. They will eagerly relay any misdemeanours to their mothers; who naturally will only have an immature narrative and no understanding of the real issues at play. This will lead to them demonising your child as they feel that his or her name crops up in their household frequently, "oh today Mummy you will never guess, Fred did...", "Our teacher got cross again today Mummy with Fred...". It may take some time but eventually this narrative will make the mother feel strongly that Fred is not a child that they want to encourage their own offspring to foster a friendship with.

They will then see the child explode from the teacher's grasp, probably tired, having tried to conform all day and overstimulated. They will then watch you chase after them in a sprint that would make Linford Christie jealous. This will confirm any suspicion. Any form of pleasantries will be suspended. I have watched a mother, when it was just the two of us at the school gates waiting for them to open, recoil in horror and desperately search for their mobile phone, rather than make eye contact, let alone conversation, with me. It always amazes me how unkind some people can be. The instant another person turns up they rush to them as if having saved them from a fate worse than death. If they only knew, and even if they do it doesn't always get better.

I've heard mothers whisper something to their friends and other mums about, how my child "lacks discipline" and is "spoiled". I'm not deaf, and I'm certainly not stupid, and neither is my child, I hear what they are saying either first hand or *via* juvenile Chinese Whispers. I think the latter is more problematic because it further erodes self-esteem. I will never forget realising my then five-year-old was begging all the mothers in turn if someday at some point, please, if they were not busy, could he please come to tea. Their replies were dismissive of him. His playdates were extremely rare occurrences, and always we were the hosts, the other children took delight in excluding him but telling him all about what was going on. It broke my heart, particularly as I had been on a charm offensive and had most of their children as guests. Don't bother trying to hope you can win friends for your child by throwing coffee and cake in the direction of people who are not going to be kind. They might love the, "free child minding" a playdate offers, but they will not reciprocate. They might also be coming to check-out how bad this naughty child really is and how poor a parent you are. They are not genuine, save your efforts, save your child and save your sanity. Your child is immature compared to theirs, something which they cannot understand, and will not behave in the way they expect.

I felt you "stare" at us from across the room. I felt you making a mental checklist of the mistakes I was making while dealing with my child's behaviour. I remember the other mothers watching in horror as my then five-year-old slid down the safety glass, (enjoying the sensory experiences the cold window had to offer), in revulsion. I could see the look of disgust on their faces. This translated into lunchtime, when no other child would sit next to him—he was 5 years old. He sat down next to a boy called Logan, who said to him, "Oh God it's you." and moved a space away, my immature child then moved up one to fill the gap; the "game" presumably went on until they had either then come full circle or another child had drawn the short straw that lunchtime. I cannot tell you the pain I felt when I discovered this, my poor boy didn't even have a soul who would sit next to him while he ate his lunch, let alone play with him after.

This isolating treatment you just witnessed is just the tip of the iceberg and you have no idea what may lie under the surface. Here's what you don't see...the parent who has had unbroken sleep akin to that of a parent of a new-born for over five or six years (and that is only going on the child's current age, it could be much longer). The child who is so frustrated that he knows he can do so much more, that he rocks in anger and uncontrollable grief at his treatment by his peer group, and you rock with him. The endless trips to specialists, school meetings, anyone who might offer support. The supplements, the diets you name it this mother has tried it. She and her child and their siblings never get any respite from it. These parents don't see that the child feels stupid, worthless, and unlovable or that they're unable to regulate any emotion and that everyday life can be difficult for them to understand and deal with. Children with ADHD are typically described as. 'young' for their years, thus an eight-year-old behaving in public like a four-year-old will raise eyebrows and other mothers will draw their conclusions.

What they cannot see is your child at home heartbroken because they have been bullied, socially isolated or excluded and they have no idea what they did wrong. This leaves the parent to try and make sense of the situation and put back together their broken child.

After the day at school your child could be just a little bit more fragmented each day than when you deposited them there. It is devastating as a mother to watch this slow erosion of the child that they are, their spark is slowly dying before you and you are powerless to do anything about it. Your child is the most wonderful creature who is fun loving, empathetic and has so much to offer, but these families cannot or will not even begin to see that.

## Playdates, parties and mothers' meetings, or the lack of them

Small or all, this is my mantra, *i.e.*, include everyone or have a tiny party. Do not exclude just one child: it is not nice. There have been countless times and I'm sure there will be more to come, where all the children in the year group have been invited to a party with the exception of one...mine! There was an, "Animal Handling" party, held by the class parent rep, who was also a teacher at the school no less. She saw fit to include all the small cohort except one—my child. The word party conjures up fun, which is naturally discussed before and after by the children in the class, these are events I have come to dread. The same lady arranged a meeting one summer holiday for all the children in Reception at a local park, unfortunately she "forgot" to inform only one family of the change in venue. I will never forget a particularly painful event where all the children in Year 4 were invited to a trampoline party, with the exception of one. I wasn't aware of this, because my son had been invited to, what I thought was a small birthday family tea at the birthday child's home. The birthday boy kindly explained when we arrived that it was, "The after party", along with another SEND child. I was horrified, and it made my child feel more different than ever. I am often very reluctant to accept party invitations unless I know the family very well. I could give you many more examples but there has to be an end to this book eventually!

The comments other parents can make: (eye roll)! You will have heard them I am sure. Here is a small selection I've had over the years and what I'd like to say in return:

"He's very lively"—No you don't say.

"I'm glad he's yours, I don't know how I'd cope"—I'm glad he's mine too!

"Boys are like dogs you have to run them"—he might seem like a wild animal but no, I don't plan on treating him like one.

"He'll grow out of it"—No you don't grow out of ADHD, it's part of who you are.

"He knows everything"—well yes, he does know a lot, he's bright, also while your family is having parties and playdates, we are at home reading books and talking with each other.

"That one's going to be a politician"—maybe, let's hope he can bring back the noose!

Have you cut out sugar/wheat/gluten/milk?" (fill in as appropriate)—Don't these people think if it was that easy, I would be doing it, and yes by the way I already have tried most of the exclusion diet?

"ADHD? I didn't know that was a real thing"—you bet it is, I have reports, books, medication and the bags under my eyes to prove it! I'm also greeted with 'it' full throttle every single morning.

"Just give him a good telling off"—ADHD children are probably the recipients of this more often than any other child I can think of— (eye roll)!

"We'd love to see you sometime, is there anywhere you can leave your son"—errrm no we're part of a team, all or nothing I'm afraid, and nothing with you, suits me best. This was said to me when my child was 18 months old.

"I completely understand how you feel, we were very worried about our son too, but he's grown out of it"—no you don't understand how I feel because as you have just said he grew out of it, and never actually got a diagnosis.

"My child has the opposite problem that he is just too popular"— what a problem to have! Not something I will ever be able to empathise with. I think this truly is a first world problem.

I could go on; I expect you have many you could add to my list and I expect I will have many more yet to come.

Plaster a smile on your face, be saccharine sweet and find your tribe.

These parents don't see the therapeutic interventions, they don't know the books you've read, the research done, or the journey you and your child are both on together. They can't understand that your child wakes up first thing in the morning full of anxiety worrying about the day ahead. They can't understand or see that you're on your knees in tears, begging for something to please help you to help your child and make it stop.

## *Your perfect child:*

There will be many occasions where your child will be perfectly happy, calm, polite, and loving. You will have tried every parenting tip and strategy out there. These parents will not understand that. They just see a terrible or weak parent spoiling their child. They see a naughty child who just needs to be properly "disciplined". They see a child who is unable to sit still, because of all the sensory input overwhelming them. They see a child who doesn't like to share, who is rude and aggressive or a child who talks all the time. A child who is badly behaved nasty, aloof and distant or who they perceive is robbing their children of their education.

They don't know you: They REALLY don't see your child at all. They are not looking.

We see a frightened, overwhelmed child who is alone, confused, struggling to cope in this environment, and who is traumatised and "stuck" in survival mode.

We see a child, who with a lots-of-love, compassion, acceptance, empathy and with time and patience, WILL grow into an amazing young adult.

When your child is successful, they will say, "if only my child had ADHD, you're so lucky." They don't really understand, no one would; yes, he's succeeding now, but it's been a long hard road.

However, there are lovely parents, teachers and amazing friends out there, it's just harder to find them. They are kind, accepting and supportive. I don't know what I would do without them; they prop me up, listen without judgement and help me see the positives in the situation. My child and I am eternally grateful to these people; they make me a better human and mother.

# SEND TOP TRUMPS AND FINDING YOUR TRIBE

An important part of looking after your child will be looking after yourself; it's like they say in aeroplanes, put on your own oxygen mask first. The same goes for your mental health. If you are off kilter then your child will be able to feel it and life will become more of a challenge for you all. There are lots of places to look for help advice and support. There are many groups set up the length and breadth of the country and with the advent of social media there are many online resources available too. As time goes on and you acquire more knowledge, you will also become a bit of an expert in the field, you will have tried many techniques and you will be best placed to help new SEN mums. The SEN world can be a bit confusing and you will need help to guide you through the processes. Remember ADHD children come in all shapes and sizes as do their parents. Not all families will be affluent, structured, cohesive this list goes on. It takes many different kinds of people to make a community, so compassion for those less fortunate and more vulnerable is a must.

Initially, it surprised me, even shocked me that there does exist a hierarchy among SEND parents. Take the time to read that again, unbelievable but true. Parents fall into several categories as they move along their individual journeys. Be careful as you go along yours; SEND parents have developed thicker skins than most but they still hurt if you jab them. I have encountered a few, which I have labelled The Ostrich, The Superior, The Judgmental and The

Herbal; they don't mean to hurt I am sure, but words do wound.

The Ostrich.

Usually, this parent has not yet got a diagnosis, or their child is about to get a diagnosis. They have a tendency to be distraught, tired and listen keenly to the answers you give them to the questions they ask, before dismissing anything ADHD related as naturally it doesn't apply to them. They may believe the paediatrician (if they have got that far) has got it wrong and their child will grow out of it. They are unaware of how hurtful and thoughtless their comments can be. They often become Herbal Parents next.

Herbal Parents.

You will have met them, maybe you were one. They are the parents that do not allow sugar, gluten and egg and have a huge array of tablets and potions in their cupboards. Their stock would be the envy of any herbal food store. They are convinced that they see no or few symptoms of ADHD in their child and are extremely against any chemical form of medication. Their children struggle as a result. These parents are tired and allude to the problems they experience, before quickly denying anything as a problem. They continue to look on you with pity and interest.

The Superior.

These parents are smug. There is no other word for it. They might not have a child with ADHD but more likely another kind of SEND. They sit there asking lots of questions, claiming they want to understand. I have found they have a tendency to forget themselves and I have even had a parent say to me, "Thank goodness it's not something awful like ADHD or ASD."

The Judgemental.

Often combined with the herbal, you medicate your child but they don't. You don't medicate your child, they do. It is sadly a case of you are dammed if you do and dammed if you don't. This is why it has to be your private family choice. This type of parents might also not believe that your child has ADHD. If you have managed your child and they are not having huge symptoms, they might feel that you are a phoney or a charlatan.

SEN top trumps

My neighbour and I are very great friends, she is supportive of me in the bad times and elated for me in the good times and I am of her too. She really is supportive of my family and especially for my neurodivergent son. Although we are some thirty years apart in age, we have one important feature in common, we are both special needs mothers. She is one of the most remarkable people I know deeply caring and compassionate. She is not a special needs mother by birth, she is a foster mother, which in my opinion makes her all the more remarkable. I am a special needs mother by birth where as she chose her daughter. She, like many people, is fascinated to find out when I first noticed that my child was not developing in the same way as his peer group, because when they had their daughter, she already knew there were significant mental health problems along with a serious and damaging history of abuse.

Both children have different comorbidities but the same diagnosis of ASD. They are divergent due to them being at opposite ends of the spectrum. This does not stop us as parents engaging in what I call "SEN Top Trumps" The needs of the individuals are clearly very different, as are the anticipated out comes for their future. The worries of us as parents are equal but very different; however, and this is important, non the less valid and anxiety inducing.

For a child who has high needs, the parents have the worry that they have no voice and that eventually, all things being equal, they will no longer be able to support their child, manage their child or ensure that their child is looked after when they are either unable to or no longer here. This is a heavy burden for these parents. To have a child who cannot manage to live independently or communicate their needs leaves them very vulnerable. However, if the child's needs are met effectively and they are looked after, the impact on the child's life is minimalised. The child's condition might be so severe that they may not yearn for friends, have no concept of the world of work or money. So long as they feel secure and their environment is managed, they may be very contented, happy and fulfilled.

A child who has less severe needs might fare differently. They might be very capable, and want to engage in and with societal norms. There is, from the child's perspective, the expectation of a job, friends and a family. If they can function to a certain extent, but are not supported and taught effectively, they may be late for work, forget to submit assignments for university applications. Not remember to pay the bills on time. They may innocently damage friendships and relationships, not knowing what they did wrong. They could be very lonely, isolated and are much more at risk of suffering severe mental health issues, such as depression and anxiety as a result. The worry for these parents is that their child might only look forward to ostracisation, isolation, relationship and financial problems.

Which child in the above two scenarios is in greater need? Which parent should worry more? Who should we think had the greater need to worry?

The answer is, both children are equal and different. Both parents have significant but differing worries for their child's future. Neither parent trumps the other.

Imagine now you come across another parent who has a severely dyslexic child. It would be very easy to think that they have fewer worries, far less than your own. Especially when the child is calm, obedient and compliant. It might be very tempting to scoff at the parents if they bemoan their worries for their child's future when you consider just getting to the school gates this morning as a herculean effort in itself. It might be that their child is at the end of primary school and can only read the Reception children's books. It might be that the parent has to organise *everything* for their child at home because they simply cannot remember the instructions. They might have worries that their child will never reach his or her potential, because they won't be able to read well enough to hold down a job commensurate with their intellectual ability. They won't cope with things, such as a bus/train time-table or fill in forms or read the menu, or be attractive to potential partners as a result. It could be that these parents look at you, an ADHD mum, and think to themselves, at least your child can be given medication and their problems are gone. At least there are doctors involved with your child's care no one cares about my child.

Who is more in need of compassion in this example? Who deserves help more?

Both families. Both children are encountering difficulties and the impact of their lives will be severe unless addressed effectively. In equal measure, the parents have significant, albeit different, concerns for their child's future. Neither family should be dismissed, neither family trumps the other. Do not fall into the trap of thinking it would be so much better if my child had... We cannot walk in someone else's shoes but we can imagine how much they might pinch.

It is all about the impact on the individual child, and eventually adult. A person who is neurodivergent who finds their niche, who is well supported will be fulfilled, happy and successful. It might take a gargantuan effort to achieve this and involve several different professionals. It will probably fill the hours you should be sleeping with worry, but it is achievable.

# CONCLUSION

On the day my son was diagnosed formally with ADHD, life felt fairly bleak; he was not quite 6 years old. I was exhausted and felt very alone. I expected his diagnosis, I even instigated the process, but, that did not stop me from grieving once it was confirmed. A part of me died that day, but a part of me was also born.

We emerged from the paediatrician's office armed with prescription and the leaflet; it was difficult to know where to look for advice and where to start first. There was so much literature, but very little that really gave me practical advice on what techniques might help us through the mire.

The literature was full of scary statistics about what appeared to be a rather bleak future. This was contrasted with pictures of successful individuals who have ADHD. I felt frightened for my son's future, but also, determined that I would do everything within my power to help him and protect him.

In the beginning I did not want to share my son's diagnosis, I felt judged and ostracised. The myth that ADHD is caused by poor parenting and that the child is simply wilful, naughty and requiring a firm hand, sadly, still persists. It is up to the ADHD community to prove to the world that this is a fallacy.

A world without ADHD would be bland and boring. ADHD people have so very much to offer and can be great company to boot.

It is important to remember that ADHD is a spectrum condition, meaning that it can be mild, severe or anywhere in between.

Although ADHD will be with you for life, it does not mean that

that life is blighted. All ADHD people are different, as individual as their non-neurodivergent counterparts.

It is caused by a chemical imbalance of neurotransmitters in the brain. It is no one's fault. Medication helps to redress this chemical imbalance it should not be used in isolation but in conjunction with strategies and support from those around the individual.

You will meet all kinds of different parents, teachers, family members, friends and experts in your journey. Be compassionate, we will never know someone's deepest worries unless they choose to share them with us. Find your tribe, school and friends might take a long time, but there are kind people out there in the meantime, "plough your own furrow".

It has been my intention in this book to demystify ADHD, empower parents, teachers and caregivers without the use of technical language, acronyms and jargon by giving practical strategies to help families and children so that they can be successful.

## References

[1] Farone, S. V., Larsson, H., *Molecular Psychiarty*, **2019**, *24*, 562

[2] Furukawa, E., Alsop, B., Sowerby, P., Jensen, S., Tripp, G., *J. Child Psychology and Psychiatry*, **2017**, *58*(3), 248

[3] Wymbs, B. T., Pelham Jr., W. E., Milina, B. S.G., Gnagy, E. M., Wilson,T. K., Greenhouse, J. B., *J. Consulting and Clin. Psycology*, **2008**, *75*(5),735

[4] Richardson, A. J., *Int. Rev. Psychiatry*, **2006**, *18*(2), 155

[5] Healing ADD: The breakthrough program that allows you to see and heal the 7 types of Attention Defficit Disorder, Berkley Pub Group, **2013**

[6] Corkum, P., Tannock, R., Moldofsky, H., *J. Am. Acad and Child Adolesc Psychiatry*, **1998**, *37*(6), 637

Printed in Great Britain
by Amazon